Invisible Riding

The secret of balance
for you and your horse

SYLVIA LOCH

A HORSE'S MOUTH PUBLICATION

Dedication

To Burma
- and to all those animals, past, present and future,
who bless us with unconditional love

First published in Great Britain in 2003
D J Murphy (Publishers) Ltd
The Horse's Mouth is an imprint of
D J Murphy (Publishers) Ltd

Text: **Sylvia Loch**

Editor: **Janet Rising**
Designer: **Jamie Powell**
Published by: **D J Murphy (Publishers) Ltd**
Haslemere House, Lower Street, Haslemere,
Surrey, GU27 2PE
Origination by **Ford Graphics Ltd**, Ringwood,
Hampshire
Printed by **The Grange Press**, Brighton,
West Sussex.

ISBN 0-9513707-7-4

Photography credits
Front cover: Hector Innes Photography.
David Miller: Pages 12, 20, 21, 26, 27, 35, 37, 39, 40, 41, 44, 47, 48, 51, 52, 55, 58,
60, 63-65, 67, 69, 70, 72, 74, 75, 79-81, 88, 91, 93, 98, 101, 102, 115.
Hector Innes Photography: Pages 15, 17, 23, 28, 30-32 32, 33, 38, 45, 53, 54, 56,
57, 61, 62, 66, 71, 73, 74, 77, 83, 86, 90, 93, 94, 95, 104, 108, 109, 114, 116, 117-121.
Lesley McDonald: Pages 82, 84.
Sylvia Loch: Pages 16, 19, 42, 46, 50, 59, 76, 87, 113, 119.
Elaine Herbert: Pages 29, 49.
Suzanne Bratten: Page 104.
Annie Wright: Page 110.

Two important caveats to all readers

1. This book is designed to help people adopt a more effective, secure and balanced position whether for dressage, hacking, or more general riding. When riding a young, immature or unmuscled horse, appropriate adaptations will need to be made (as explained within the text) in order to adopt a lighter, more forward seat. Clearly, for any form of jumping the same rule will apply. When in doubt, seek professional advice.

2. Neither the author nor the publishers can be held responsible for any injury or damages, howsoever arising, caused directly or indirectly as a result of following text, instructions or methods in this book. This book is written for people who can already ride, but who wish to move on to improving their understanding and technique.

Contents

Introduction
Invisible riding for everyone

"A horseman is said to have light aids when his movements are subtle and not too obvious, and while maintaining the proper balance, he guides his horse with competence and ease: this is also called hidden aids"....

École de Cavalerie by Sieur de la Guérinière, 1733

Few of us like to ride a horse and not feel in control. Horses are bigger and much more powerful than us and, as creatures of flight, are not always predictable. How, therefore, can we be sure of developing a method of riding that allows us to remain comfortable, effective and, above all, safe?

Judging by the amount of controlling and generally restrictive tack that we see on the average horse these days, few riders have any real faith in their own capabilities. Many seem to prefer to trust their equipment instead of their own bodies. They place stronger and stronger bits in the horse's mouth, tighten the noseband beyond the comfort zone, and even resort to gadgets which force an energetic or willful horse into an artificial shape or outline. All this is virtually resorting to tug-of-war tactics, which can be enormously damaging to the horse's mouth, neck and back. It may also ruin his natural balance and, even worse, his goodwill. There are too many angry and damaged horses about these days as a result of forceful riding of this kind.

The power within us
Wouldn't it be nice if we could dispense with the gadgets and discover a power within our bodies to help us cope with the most awkward horse or situation – and all without stress? How much easier riding would be if, before allowing the energy of the horse to escape or get ahead of us, we could control or channel it from its source, i.e. the moment it leaves the hindquarters. *"Don't be silly!"* I hear you say; *"Whoever heard of that! If that were possible, surely everyone would be doing it!"*

But the truth is they are not. Indeed, most riders are totally unaware that they even have this power, and certainly few people seem able

Riding should be stress-free – for both horse and rider!

to teach it. Whilst really talented riders possess this ability, they are not necessarily aware of what they do, or even that it is a natural thing. They may just think they are blessed with a very special gift, believing there is no way they can pass it on to others.

The first step on the path

Yet I believe we all have a chance to use and develop the gift of empowerment, whatever our shape and size, whatever our discipline. Over the years, I have helped countless ordinary riders with ordinary horses to grasp it but, unless one really wants to ride in a better way and in partnership, it simply won't happen. Once we recognise this and open our minds to the possibilities, we're already one step forward on the path. Obviously, some will find it easier than others, but there is no reason why everyone should not have the chance to develop to the best of their ability the various techniques this brings. That is why I have written this book. I want to help other people to tune into the power of their own bodies by using their mind and their understanding to bring these natural effects into play. These are the tools for invisible riding.

A two-way thing

There is no doubt that organised, empathetic and effective riding is very much a question of mind-over-matter. But that it not enough on its own. We have to align ourselves so that we ourselves are in a position to establish the basic balance so necessary for the horse to be in balance under us. This means sitting in such a way that we are absolutely central to the horse, our weight resting over the strongest part of his body (see *The Classical Seat**). Improving technique will start off as a two-way thing – horse to rider, rider to horse – but should eventually merge into a process that becomes semi-automatic. This is the state of riding that we wish to aspire to, and is what most people describe as 'feel'. How often do we hear people say, *"He has great feel with his horses,"* or the student who says *"Can you help me develop feel?"*

Yet feel is not magic; it comes from years of practice and mental application. And without first thinking, it's impossible to use our body to greater effect. We have to know what we want and believe that it is perfectly possible, before we enable the physical process to take place. For example, when we wander down the aisle of a supermarket and mentally note that we need a tin of soup, a pack of butter, a bag of peas, we must realise that none of these things will find their way into our trolley unless we register that we want them! The actual picking up and placing them in the trolley requires very little effort at all, it is the thinking and knowing exactly what we want which sets the process in motion.

That's how it should be in riding; the power of the mind enables the power of the body to carry out the most simple or the most complex physical things with ease. In other words, there's no big deal! We can go through the physical actions as though we had done nothing. Finally this will become instinctive, but we have to start the process first. This is what I mean when I talk about power. We all have it - it's just a question of registering what we want and knowing HOW to allow it to happen....

So read on - invisible riding is for everyone!

The Classical Seat by Sylvia Loch, available from D J Murphy (Publishers) price £9.99.

Chapter One

Tuning in

In Nature, freedom and personal space are probably even more important to the horse than food and warmth. His safety depends on it. If, therefore, we could learn to ride in such a way that the horse still feels he enjoys some freedom – in his gaits, in his back, in his mouth – a much more willing partnership might emerge. Instead of feeling trapped or stressed, a horse ridden in such a way would accept his work much better, whilst a huge potential for co-operation and versatility could be developed. Riding in this way will not deny us control. On the contrary, it can provide us with even more, but in a manner which invites the horse to offer it.

A matter of balance

Most people know that the energy of the horse starts in the hind end. The quarters and hindlegs are often referred to as the engine of the horse and it is this which drives him forward. As a result we should feel his energy flowing through to the front end where it is harnessed via the bit into our hands. We call this 'contact', and, depending upon the mode and level of training, the contact can either be sure and soft, hesitant or uneven, or even pulling and hard.

Generally speaking, the more the weight of the horse is transferred into the shoulders or forehand, the heavier he will feel in our hands,

Balancing a very forward-going horse through the centre means we can retain good control through a light, easy rein.

which is very tiring for the rider. If, however, we can retain his weight at the centre – or in the more advanced horse transfer it towards the rear – the lighter the contact, the more pleasant the riding.

Since all this is a matter of balance, resorting to stronger aids and gadgets which deal with the front end is like bolting the stable door after the horse has escaped. Instead, we should concentrate on riding in such a way that we can retain and control the balance long before it tips beyond that point of no return.

Nature's aids

Everyone knows that our natural aids are those of our bodies, generally described as those of the seat, leg and hand. However, how many recognise that, in applying each and every aid, a shifting or redistribution of our own bodyweight is involved? Even small shifts can affect the horse's balance and these can either work for or against us. The trick is to know what does what!

Through trial and error, most riders discover the general principle that the horse will always try to move or balance under our weight, in order to catch us. In the same way that a man carrying a heavy sack will step under it if it swings away — thus avoiding a loss of balance – the horse will always try to step under our weight for the same reason. This is as much out of self-preservation as goodwill!

Clearly, therefore, if we tip forward with heavy shoulders, the horse will tend to do the same. The more we lean, the more he will try to catch up. The more the jockey crouches and takes his weight forward, the more the horse flattens out to follow suit. By contrast, the dressage rider sitting in the vertical, concentrates his bodyweight over the centre of the horse to keep the horse more together and 'under' him. Many people would call this basic common sense, but these scenarios are important to analyse, since, in a much more refined sense, the principle of balancing weight forms the basis of all the aids – it provides the language by which we speak to our horse.

Once we accept the influence of a centred or central position, there are endless adjustments and changes we can make while hacking, schooling, jumping and so on. For most of the time we will want to keep the horse more 'under' us. This allows us to indicate differences of direction, impulsion, outline and

This rider has never had a dressage lesson in her life, but her natural instinct to deepen her weight fractionally right helps in the turn.

gait in the most immediate and effortless way e.g. rein-back to canter, hand-canter to full gallop, gallop to trot, turn, a few short steps in front of an obstacle, canter to walk and so on.

In other words, by balancing the horse from the centre, we can work on the horse's energy long before it reaches the extremities. In this way, we can conserve or release impulsion, making it available as and when we want it. By working this way, we can develop responses which over the weeks, months and years, will give us tremendous powers over the body of the horse, but all in a quiet, apparently effortless way – which is much nicer for him.

But first, we need to understand the logic behind this language. There are many contradictions in riding and we need to be aware of what works positively for the horse (and us), and what works negatively. Indeed, often what would seem like a good idea is actually the

Left: Clinging on with the leg leads to restriction elsewhere; the horse is pressured sideways and the rider tightens through the whole body. Right: 'Letting go' with the leg frees up both horse and rider.

wrong one – but it's important we understand why! For this reason, each chapter of this book will examine the different aids in turn, but we must remember that no aid should ever be given in isolation. Just like the horse, our whole body needs to work seamlessly, and as one.

Weight aids

What are weight aids? Because this term is used in Western riding, but rarely heard in the average riding school, people seem to think of these as something rather specialised, foreign or different. Yet the weight aids are nothing more than the end result of the conventional aids, but it's how we apply these that introduces the idea of bodyweight or pressure. And it's this pressure, or lack of it, which can make such a huge difference to what is felt by the horse. For example:

● squeezing with the leg shifts a proportion of our weight against the horse's side which may

change or restrict his action;
● pushing hard with the legs against the stirrup increases pressure in the back of the rider's seatbones and thighs, which may cause the horse to tense and rush forward;
● letting go with the leg and allowing weight merely to drop into the stirrup frees the horse to move forward, while the downward pressure in the stirrup helps maintain balance.
Three completely different feels, three totally different effects!

In this way, every action we make may give the horse a completely different feel or command. So whether we are turning or bending a joint, flexing or relaxing muscles, drawing up or letting down, raising an arm here, dropping a leg there, leaning a little this way or that, we are inadvertently shifting weight which may radically change the pressures and, in consequence, the balance.

Having established, therefore, that the term

'weight aid' is nothing more than a clarification of what the horse is feeling under saddle at any given moment, it's easy to imagine how mistakes can be made. With our head weighing about 10 pounds, and the upper body several more, slouching, leaning back or wobbling about can be very disturbing to the horse's equilibrium. So can constantly squeezing or flapping legs.

Hacking out

Riding across country in canter or gallop, the horse will feel much more secure and confident with a 'natural' rider – someone who automatically knows how to balance himself over the centre of gravity and can remain there quietly and easily. On the other hand, a less adept rider may move his weight all over the place with dire results. Instead of setting himself up to give the horse a lead, every change in terrain makes him lean this way and that and the horse, having constantly to compensate, may risk a fall. It is sad when people blame the horse and seem totally unaware that their own lack of balance and body control brings this about.

Out on the roads, it should be obvious that the rider who sits up tall, quiet and vertical, and whose horse responds to discreet leg aids, will not only have a more pleasant, lighter ride, she will have much more control. But how often do we see this? Too many riders sit slumped, as though they're watching television, with the horse, in consequence, slopping along on the forehand. Horses like these, often hollowing away from an unbalanced seat, will be much harder to correct in the event of a sudden emergency.

Whatever we are doing we should never forget that the way in which we distribute our bodyweight will directly affect the horse's spinal column. This in turn will affect his ability to engage or disengage, which ultimately influences all his movement. A horse ridden more 'together' can react immediately to us. The disconnected horse cannot – so, from a safety point of view, vital seconds may be lost. There is no doubt that a horse which is continually ridden with negative weight aids – often the result of over-riding and pushing – learns to harden himself to the aids and simply switches off. This could be life-threatening when riding out.

Balance is the key

If all this sounds unrealistic, let us examine the whole idea of balance in the simplest way possible. Balancing a pole on your shoulder so that you can move forward easily and with confidence involves adjusting that pole to get the weight evenly distributed. The difference between getting the pole just into balance or just out of balance is, however, very slight – but it can make a difference to your task. For the horse it is much the same. Life would be much happier if he could balance the rider in the optimum place for himself, but unfortunately he rarely has any say in the matter for it is the rider who is 'in the driving seat'. That is why we need to set ourselves up to help him. In other words, we become his balancing pole. Because of our shape we should think of this in the vertical rather than the horizontal.

Staying in balance and, more importantly in schooling, asking our horse to balance under us, requires an awareness of how gravity works. This involves being able to adjust weight commensurate with how the horse is moving, but without removing that central pole of support. Since every movement is different, and the way in which we want it performed may be different, each request will be slightly different. We must never remove all the points of reference at once. That is why in turning right, for example, we may slightly (and correctly) weight the right seat bone, but tilting or collapsing right could well have the opposite effect!

On the ground, we make adjustments unconsciously and easily. Balancing on a plank or even balancing on one foot should not require overt compensation by the rest of the body, but to look at some riders on a circle you would think the opposite. It is well worth, therefore, exploring your balancing capabilities on the ground, since all of us have a tendency to favour one side. If we are to become good, 'feeling' riders and encourage our horses to perform to optimum level with invisible aids, we need to improve our own balance in and out of the saddle.

Changing balance by adjusting our distribution of weight is more to do with thinking and feeling when it is right, rather than doing. That's how it should be on horseback, too.

This stout pole can be balanced easily by Sylvia's daughter Allegra once she centres herself under its weight.

Allegra experiments with shifting her weight by minute stages until what was out of balance suddenly comes fully into balance. It is simply a matter of feel, supporting upward, and thinking central!

Still erect, Allegra finds it easy to balance on her left leg, even though her right leg swings freely in the air. In riding we may concentrate our weight in similar fashion to direct our horse to right or to left. The old masters described the inside leg as a pillar for the horse to bend around.

Minimalist riding

At the other extreme is the happy, well-ridden horse whose education and correct schooling has allowed him to become 'sensitised' to the smallest adjustments. Since gravity is such a powerful force, the good rider will realise that all the weight shifts or aids should be used sparingly so that you would have to look hard to notice them. Invisible, minimalist riding is therefore the key to success.

This process of sensitising the horse can only develop correctly, however, if we ourselves are consistent with each and every request. This requires that we educate ourselves to become more aware of exactly how, when, where and *why* we are doing things. Once we recognise these effects, we can develop our aids to the point where the horse becomes so attuned that the slightest turn of the head, a minute deepening of the appropriate seat bone, or the softening of the tummy muscles, can bring about the desired response.

However, as with all things concerned with balance, subtlety is the name of the game. Looking at the picture opposite, minute adjustments, such as deepening the inside seatbone to hold the horse in a gentle bend right, would improve the whole picture. This would, in turn, fractionally drop the rider's right seatbone, which in turn would make it easier for her to deepen and support her horse through the inside leg (which is turning out). Allowing the outside shoulder to advance gently would also help, but again we are talking about the minutiae.

Remember, it only took one straw to change the load on the camel's back from bearable to unbearable. Similarly, by removing pressure, the camel could work again. With the average riding lesson placing too much on doing and not enough on allowing, it is hardly surprising when people and horses get confused. Remember, it's often when we change or take off the pressure that the horse – like the camel — is motivated to offer more.

From a good central balance, the horse can be sensitised to minimal changes in our bodyweight to bring about dramatic results.

Because the horse is wider through the quarters than the forehand, he will need a little more help from the rider to enable him to track up straight.

One sidedness

The more things you try, the more you will discover imbalances and weaknesses. This becomes very obvious when we ski, skate or skateboard, but even for quite mundane things we all have a tendency to favour one side. If we can appreciate this before we ride we will have increased our general awareness and be far less likely to blame the horse when things go wrong. More importantly, understanding these failings enables us to correct ourselves.

Self assessment

Here are some questions to help you discover which side you favour for some quite simple tasks.
- **When running upstairs, which leg do you generally push off with?**
- **Which leg prefers to lead when you skip?**
- **Can you balance as easily on one foot as the other?**
- **When standing and chatting to a friend, which hip are you likely to collapse?**
- **Which leg do you prefer to hop on?**
- **With or without a hula hoop, which way round would you feel happy rotating your hips – clockwise or anti-clockwise?**
- **If you are throwing a ball from one hand to the other, which hand prefers to throw and which to catch?**
And so on.

You might not think the answer to any of these questions could relate to your riding, but it does! One side of you will prefer to receive and be more passive, the other side will prefer to take charge, push and be more active. Think, therefore, how this may affect your horse! Almost without exception, people who are very active with the right side of the body will have a horse that falls out through the left shoulder. He may be reluctant to canter right, and he could be more stiff on the left rein. All this is a logical response to the rider's right-sidedness, and we are not only talking about the hands. Even if you yourself are not very one-sided, your horse's previous rider may have been.

Off balance

Blaming the horse or blaming ourselves is counterproductive. No horse is totally ambidextrous and I have yet to find a rider who is l00 per cent consistent throughout the body – none of us are perfect! It may also be heartening to know that often the most experienced people apply their weight incorrectly. I have seen this when people book to have a lesson on one of my more advanced schoolmasters and the look of surprise – even horror – when the horse goes off on three tracks and in the opposite direction when all they wanted was to turn onto a straight line, is revealing. A shoulder-in or leg yield looks very nice when correctly requested; but when it results from overloading one seat bone or leg aid, embarrassment follows! What makes things worse in severe cases, is the rider's inability to correct things. This is largely because they have never been made aware of exactly where they are going wrong. So many trainers focus on the horse instead of the rider and many students will have difficulty relating to their own bodies.

With other peoples' horses, I find similar problems. Whilst the older horses try their best, but are stiff and one sided, the novice horses simply do not understand. Too many riders are asking for things in the wrong way and thinking it is the horse's fault when he can not give it to them. They find it mind-boggling when it is explained that their own aids have made it impossible for their horse even to begin to answer their request. The most common mistakes include;
- pushing weight downward and against – instead of freeing up;
- pushing weight backward – when they really mean forward;
- pushing weight against – when they mean the horse to turn in;
- pressuring the horse with both legs at once so that his energy gets blocked through the middle – rather than letting it flow through!

Because of these mistakes, I have seen the horse's natural action being sacrificed time and time again. Where there should be freedom and impulsion, I see shortened, constricted gaits and a stuffy attitude to work. When I talk about the weight aids, a vague, uncomprehending look creeps into the rider's eyes. Often, the only way to neutralise the rider's aids is to ask for rising trot, which allows them to take the pressure off.

Seven fundamentals

So before we clarify these matters step-by-step, let us highlight what we have discussed so far;
● the horse needs us to be his balancing pole;
● he needs help – i.e. our aids – to balance around us;
● every aid involves a shift in weight and pressure;
● every aid can change the balance;
● if any aid is applied over frequently or forcefully, it blurs the whole – how often do we hear of horses being 'dead to the legs'?
● for him to 'listen' again we need invisible, minimalist aids;
● by 'allowing' as much as possible we give the horse a chance to move!

Switching the horse back on

To sum up, I am always somewhat wary when I hear about brain-dead, stubborn or insensitive horses, for such an animal is rare in the larger scheme of things. What generally happens is that the horse switches off when given the wrong signal, or worse, is overloaded with too many conflicting aids all applied at once. Generally speaking, as you ask with one aid, you should be slightly giving with the other. Too much 'doing' all the time will cause confusion.

One thing we should never forget – it's in the horse's nature to move, and most really do like to move! But no horse likes to move out of balance, in pain or in discomfort! How we ask our horses to move therefore should be much more a matter of re-channelling, rather than making! The softly-softly approach will restore the horse's feeling and listening powers again and the most hardened cases can be transformed under a sympathetic, subtle rider. If you want to know how....read on!

Tuning into gravity leads to a happy, confident and balanced horse.

Chapter Two

Forward with ease!

In former times, there was a fairly uniform method of teaching riders and schooling horses, and the two went hand-in-hand. Wise, schoolmaster horses that had already been sensitised by top level riders were given to novice riders to learn from. In this way, the horses in turn showed their pupils the different 'feels' by obeying when the pressures were right, and disregarding or doing the opposite when the pressures were wrong. Gradually, the pupil learned from the horse where or where not to use the leg, how and how not to open or close the hand, and just how much push or lightening with the seat was acceptable.

Coupled with the observational powers of the instructor, this worked very well. Over a period of time these methods were developed and passed on to future riders who taught future horses in the same way.

Based on logic

In days gone by, these methods were known as classical. For classical read 'natural' since the whole philosophy of riding this way is based on logic – ie adhering to Nature's laws of balance, gravity, locomotion, etc.

Today, too many riders are confused by instructions which they find difficult to understand. *"Make your horse do this, make him do that! Don't let him do this, don't let him do that!"* But what if you don't know how or why? If this cannot be explained simply and easily, such instruction may well prove valueless.

Judging from my mail bag, there are many concerned owners who would clearly like to ride better, but feel the techniques they have read about, or are told to carry out, are beyond them. Often, there is conflicting advice. Worse, whichever method they follow, they seem unable to get through to their horse. The truth is, if we don't understand the reasoning behind a certain course of action, it's highly unlikely our horse will respond in the way we want.

Since the horse looks to us as a herd leader, unwillingness and a lack of trust can become a real problem. Horses need confident riders to work well, so surely it's up to us to open the lines of communication and start again. It would be the greatest tragedy if we lost the art of knowing how to communicate with our horse just because we were afraid to ask.

We might start by asking

● Are my schooling methods based on logic?
● Does the same method work with every horse I ride?
● Do they relate to what I myself can (or can't) do on the ground?
● Do I always do things in the same particular way?
● Do I understand why I ask in that particular way?
● Am I convinced my horse understands?
● Is he able to go on doing something after I've asked without me continually nagging at him?

If the answer to any of these questions is 'no' – please read on!
If the answer to the last question is 'no', we might also ask ourselves –
● Do I reward my horse (by easing the aid) at every stage to reinforce his understanding?
● Do I reward with my
    a) hand?
    b) leg?
    c) seat?
    d) voice?
    e) general demeanour?
Not necessarily all at the same time!

As the horse offers more from behind, we should reinforce his understanding of forwardness by rewarding and easing off pressure with both the rein and the leg.

Clearly, before expecting anything of our horses, we should always look to ourselves.

Contradictory terms

Quite apart from the different methods and schools of thought that abound in today's world of sporting riding, there are also many contradictions in terms. Let us examine the way in which the aids are often described, one by one.

LEGS The book says that we should close the legs to go forward, but a few pages later, we read that closing the legs is appropriate for halt!

Is there an in-between stage? How can we show the horse the difference?

SEAT The use of the seat seems just as confusing. Many teachers say 'push down' to stop, yet a moment later we are told to push again to make the horse go forward. Often, we see horses being pushed and pulled at the same time. From a logical point of view a 'push' sounds quite invasive, so is it realistic to expect that continuous pushing will make the horse more willing?

HANDS This brings us to the whole question of contact. Many instructors insist upon a closed

Pushing and pulling at the same time! This is not how my student normally rides, but you would be surprised how many people think this is the way to stop or slow a horse, or even put him on the bit!

fist for both halt and forward. If this is so, how is the horse to know the difference between stop and go?

Of course, there are logical answers to all the above questions which show that riding technique is not as contradictory as at first supposed. But unless we ourselves understand these nuances and shades of difference, we will only confuse our horse. Ears back, teeth grinding, head shaking, tail swishing etc, are all signs of a confused or distressed horse.

Clearly, the only way forward is to take the aids to their logical conclusion and try to feel

just what each aid does and how it influences the horse. This brings us back to the whole idea of pressure and weight, without which there can be no meaningful aid or request.

If all this sounds revolutionary, we should remember that guidance in these matters has been at hand for centuries. It was Xenophon, the ancient Greek cavalry commander, who first explained that we should ride in the same balance as though standing on our own two feet with our legs bent and apart. In more modern times we hear instructors saying *"Imagine what would happen if the horse was swept out from*

Off the horse!

One of the best ways in which these different feels and sensations can be developed is by recognising and practising the weight aids on the ground. This has led to my giving unmounted weight aid clinics all over the UK and beyond, to increase awareness of feel so we can apply the aids correctly for the horse, and in a way that works on his natural instincts. It may sound bizarre, but making transitions or walking, jogging or skipping circles, corners, straight lines, etc ourselves, really does help us tune in to what the horse will require from us.

Indeed, after a mere two to three hour session in an indoor group situation, the difference when these students return to the saddle is truly breathtaking. A one-off dismounted lesson really can change one's whole perception of riding and last a lifetime. The methods involved can be extended to all horses and all riders of all disciplines. From basic forward work to canter pirouette and flying changes, we can see what will work on the horse's body and what will not. This gives students the tools for their future schooling and provides an answer to virtually every question they may ever have wanted to ask.

The truth is – on or off the horse – we are all influenced by the same laws of gravity, but only when we have learned to tune into these, can they really be made to work for us and the horse

Rising trot allows us to balance better by connecting us to gravity through the stirrups; this helps us to free up through the leg and seat, which in turn helps the horse.

under you, would you land in balance on the ground?"

The main message from this philosophy is that we, as riders, owe it to ourselves and to the horse to take responsibility for our own weight. This is sometimes called centred or balanced riding, but the idea is the same. Therefore, whether we ride with short stirrups for jumping, longer stirrups for dressage, or something in between for hacking and trail riding, we should still be able to support much of our bodyweight with own two feet. This immediately puts us in touch with our in-built sense of gravity – our feet have sensors which tell us exactly where we are in space.

From the horse's point of view, the more we take our weight into the stirrup, the more we should spare his back. Obviously, whatever the position we adopt, the horse still has to bear however many pounds we weigh. However, since

Piggy-back proof

Anyone who has ever carried a younger brother or sister on their back will recognise the difference between supported and unsupported weight. The slumped, wriggly, pushing child is murder to carry! The one who sits still, opens the shoulders and supports themselves upward and forward, allows you to get on with the job of carrying. Not only can a loose, floppy body feel awkward, it will also feel heavier, since it is virtually dead weight.

This brings another factor into the equation – and that is air! We all know that a balloon or lilo that has run out of air simply collapses inertly on the ground. One that is full of air lightens immediately and, in the case of the balloon, takes off! Yet the material or skin of the two objects weighs exactly the same whether empty or inflated. It is the same with us. When we sit up, open our shoulders, breathe properly and allow our upper body to expand, we make ourselves light for the horse. If, on the other hand, we sit slumped, hunched or crumpled, we become heavy lumps, swayed this way and that by the movement of the horse, and a real burden to carry.

If you don't believe me (and don't have a back problem) experiment for a moment and give someone a piggy-back and feel for yourself. Allow them to go floppy and deflated, then ask them to sit up and breathe! At the end of the day, awareness is everything and the horse himself will generally indicate what is correct for him.

Allegra weighs eight-and-a-half stone, but when she sits up and supports her back, it's relatively easy for me to stay erect and carry her. As in riding, she needs to be just forward of the vertical for me to move forward easily. If she slumped, I would definitely slump on the forehand!

the stirrups are slung relatively close to the front of the saddle, weight-bearing is easiest when we are in the forward seat, as then we are over the strongest part of the equine back. That is why we shorten our stirrups for jumping and cross country – to give ease and freedom of movement to a relatively vulnerable back.

If, on the other hand, we ride with too long a stirrup or bareback the horse tends to take the rider's weight further back towards the weaker spot. This is bearable when riders have very good balance and know how to support themselves through the upperbody; it can be pretty unbearable however, if the rider is crooked, out of sync and slipping back.

Think connected!

Before we leave the subject of supporting weight, never forget the role of our joints in riding. The only thing that alters according to the different lengths of stirrup will be the angles of the body. And, as every good downhill ski-er knows, you need angles to absorb shock.

So whether you are jumping, galloping or sitting a sedate trot, never forget that contact through the ball of the foot on the stirrup bar allows our ankles, knees, hips, shoulders and elbows to flex and act as shock absorbers. This is especially relevant in the rising trot, but it is a mistake not to utilise all the joints when we sit deeply, too. Soft ankles, mobile knees and supple hips all have their part to play whatever type of riding we do, and it is a known fact that the rider's back will not 'swing' if the rest of the body is not pliable too.

Through downward pressure (which ultimately connects us to the ground) we have a great tool with which to steady ourselves and the horse from a greater sense of support underneath. This is due to the amazing ability of our joints to block and to hold, as well as to give. Again, good riders do this quite unconsciously, whilst others need to be made aware.

Learning to utilise gravity not only helps us to control and disperse our weight, it makes everything much nicer and easier for the horse – providing us with a fantastic, but wholly natural method of control. Once you learn and feel this, you will never forget it.

Just to highlight the importance of downward pressure into a contacting surface beneath, think by comparison how you would feel hanging from the ceiling with your legs off the floor! That

Our stirrups can also be used to steady the horse. It's just a matter of using those joints!

is how some people ride, they're just hanging in here with little idea of what they are missing. Basically, unless you are a trapeze artist, losing your 'connection' to the ground makes your body horribly cumbersome and out of control. Only by connecting into gravity do we have the power to control our muscles, work the joints and move in harmony. This is one of the main principles of all movement, yet because they are sitting on a moving animal, too many people forget it.

It just doesn't happen!

One of the worst things we can do in riding is to try too hard. Your attitude may be correct but if you try to force things you can so easily desensitise and block your horse. Our method of riding is designed to liberate your horse, but you may need to keep reminding yourself of this fact.

When we over-ride, the majority of horses respond by switching off. Ask yourself – did I ask and wait for it to happen, or did I keep asking, so it couldn't happen? In such an event, simply try again, one step at a time – and remember, less is more. Remember too, that a strong aid can create such an imbalance that the horse feels safer not to try – or does the opposite! This happens more often than you would think and is shown in the following ways:

● a reluctance to go forward;
● an inability to bend one way (or the other – or both) on the circle;
● an inability to stand still at halt;
● running on in trot, instead of cantering;
● falling into trot, after canter;
● changing legs or going disunited round a corner;
● a reluctance to rein-back.... and so on. The list can be endless.

Too many trainers spend hours trying to correct the horse for problems such as these, when it is clearly the fault of the rider. Do we tinker with the engine when the car stalls? Or do we try to improve the understanding of the person in the driving seat? It should be the same in riding.

Energy flow

With my own pupils, I find it very helpful to liken the energy of a horse to the flow of a river as it passes through a channel. The banks of the river are represented by the riders' legs and hands. As long as these remain quietly passive, uniform, forward-looking and stable, an even flow of forward energy can be maintained. However, once one side gives way or opens sideways, energy can be diverted outwards and away from the main channel. The river banks

Extended trot. A quick close and release with the leg at the girth helps to promote an extravagant medium trot

can also narrow together or deepen to create greater 'spurt' at a given point; by closing in partially or fully however, they will dampen or stop the energy.

In addition to the banks of the river, there is a further channelling effect overhead. This takes the form of a bridge-type structure which is represented by our seat and upper body. Again, this can be opened up to allow the river to pass more freely underneath, or it can lower to cause

Collected trot. The leg which partially closes and absorbs energy will promote a more collected gait.

through the upper body, seat and leg. On a lazy horse, the idea is to activate the hindlegs so the river may be sent on its way, and once we free up ourselves the horse is encouraged to follow by example. Think of the aids in the following terms:

SEAT AND UPPER BODY This is the bridge/lock or dam over the river. It must open enough to allow the river to pass through but not enough to cause a torrent; it must also know how to 'take or collect', ie harness or gather energy

LEGS The upper thigh, and knee in particular, represent the river banks. They must know how much to steady support, re-channel. The lower legs must know how much to ask, encourage and allow – remember, narrowing the gap can also create greater 'spurt' (as in a hosepipe), but only if we have enough energy to utilise!

HANDS These control the approach to the mouth of the river – the point at which it reaches its destination. They must know how

Allowing forward with the upper body, seat, legs and hand will encourage the energy to be carried through to the forehand.

a reduction or dampening down of forward flow. Finally, it can even be turned into a dam by closing down altogether. If the structure inadvertently collapses it may also block the energy flow.

How to interact

Once riders begin to visualise the horse's energy in terms of a river, the framework of the aids and how we interact makes more sense. As you ride try to feel and become aware...

● ...that the source of the river is in the hindquarters

● ...that the current travels forward and over your horse's back

● ...that once the energy reaches the mouth of the river – the forehand – it may start to disperse

● ... how through gentle gathering (further channelling) it can be recycled to its source.

On an energetic horse, the trick is to be able to keep the energy from disappearing 'through the front door'. This is done by absorbing energy

Absorbing upwards through a more toned upper body, and gently checking seat, leg and hand, centralises the energy and leads to greater balance.

much to yield – yielding too much may allow a rush (onto the forehand); they must also know how much to retain – without blocking the flow – so that the energy-making properties of the entire river can be recycled back to its source.

The idea is not to let all the energy arrive in the hands, but to keep the river flowing in a cyclical way so that the power from the hindquarters is absorbed through the rider's body. Thus it can be regenerated for whatever purpose - forward, lateral, collected, extended, upward, and even backward movement.

By exploring these ideas, we should begin to appreciate how fine and feeling the aids should be. Thinking like this puts us in tune with the horse's instinctive forces. Every time he shows us that he has understood, it should be clear what needs to happen next. Gradually, he will teach us never to ask in an inappropriate way. The test of our own efficacy is that our horse – any horse – understands us and does things easily.

Will all this work for me?

The answer to the above question has to be yes! yes! yes! But you must be prepared to open your mind and self-assess in everything you require from your horse. When things go wrong, there are too many riders who automatically think the horse has misunderstood. With these methods, you will have to turn your thinking around and assume the mistake lies with yourself.

This may have to happen up to 20 or even 30 times in a schooling session, but once you begin to question and work out why it was your horse could not offer what was required, you – as a rider – will develop greater awareness and improvement will follow. In this way, your horse can become your best teacher and will teach you by showing you how not to do things as well as how to do them.

Providing a framework for our horse's energy allows us to feel what he feels, and know where to support and where to allow.

Chapter Three

Transitions
- the seat and upper body

We have already discussed the idea of discovering and recognising the weight aids, which are so important as a means of communication to the horse. Simply by tuning into the sensation of gravity which flows downwards and works through all of us, we can learn much greater control of movement, whatever we are doing. We have also discussed how our stirrups will help to support and stabilise us when we ride, sparing the horse's back and enabling us to absorb movement though our joints. Unfortunately, not everyone uses the stirrups appropriately.

In riding we should strive for what works for us on the ground. Here, with hips forward and a proud upper body posture, I can lighten my step and move in good balance.

What goes wrong?

Granted, it is generally taught nowadays that if the rider is unable to keep the heel roughly under her hips, balance will be lost. However, corrections are often made in such a way that they do more harm than good. Examples are as follows:

● **Many riders sit to the rear of the saddle instead of finding the central point.**
● **Having mounted, they immediately grip with their legs which pulls up the knees, shooting** them towards the cantle.
● **Settling back into the most comfortable part of the saddle, they then collapse the upper body and adopt a chair seat.**

The instructor recognises that the rider is unlikely to stay in place with bottom back and feet stuck forward, but instead of correcting the

Many people think that by relaxing down into the horse, they will make it easier for him. The contrary is true! Collapsing the abdominals and dropping the diaphragm will lead to uneven weight pressure, which may block the horse and lead to crookedness.

rider's hips, lower back and upper body position, they take the easy way out and simply pull the rider's legs back. This may or may not bring the rider's seat more towards the centre of the saddle, but it's not good enough.

If the rider is stiff through the back, what happens next – to accommodate the leg position – is that they either ...

● ...tip forward onto the fork with a hollow back, – or
● ...collapse the ribcage and pelvis, and round the back.

Now everyone is happy (except the horse); the rider can keep their feet under them and the instructor proudly points out that the hip-to-heel alignment has been achieved. However, such a position puts the rider's weight against the horse, hampering smooth forward movement, with all the rider's energy directed in a negative way. The rider then resorts to stronger driving aids, often combined with incessant kicking.

To achieve a classical position, The Spanish Riding School firstly work riders on the lunge with a stick placed between the elbows to encourage the natural flexion of the lower back. My own pupils generally benefit from hands-on help to demonstrate how the upward support of the abdominal 'core' muscles allows the back to inflex without over-hollowing. In turn, this allows the sheer weight of the seat and leg to drop snugly into place.

Think up and forward!

For good, forward flatwork, we need to support ourselves upwards (more or less vertically) to neutralise the position of our pelvis. This in turn raises our centre of gravity and releases dead weight pressure from the horse's back.

Since acceleration will tend to push us backwards, a good way to remain central is to think of riding 'waist to hands'. Consolidating our balance in this way also frees the horse's back from stifling pressure, and there is much greater ease of movement.

Sitting tall allows the legs to hang in a draped fashion. Once the knees drop away, the muscle fibres of the thigh lengthen out and we can apply the forward aids with the lower leg uncontracted but toned. Again, this gives the horse a feeling of release since the lack of contraction allows gravity to flow through us and out again without getting 'stuck' along the way. Once the horse becomes sensitised to this

feeling of greater freedom and less interference from above, he becomes more attentive to small changes. It's almost a thinking matter to apply a momentary weight aid willingly to interrupt the forward flow.

For a great 'centred' position

To channel energy correctly, it is time to reconsider what the classical riding masters taught us.

● The rider must advance the hips (pelvis) in a vertical position to bring him/her as close as possible to the pommel – the strongest part of the horse's back;
● a proud upper body posture with shoulders back allows the rider's core muscles to support and maintain forward flexion of the loins (lower back);
● this stabilises the seat vertically, which allows the hip joint to 'open' so the leg can fall away and around the horse;
● once the thigh muscles are unconstricted, the thigh and knee can drop to adhere easily to the saddle;
● with stirrups hanging vertically, the lower leg can also soften and drop;
● the rider's heel can now align easily under the hip so the whole rider is in balance;
● this allows the rider to sit up and 'let go' with the weight;
● pressure on the ball of the foot will secure the stirrup – not through pushing, but merely through gravity.

This 'connected' feeling allows the rider to sit deeply, but never heavily. It enables the seat to absorb movement without losing stability. Quiet, but in control, we are now at one with the horse. Indeed, we have become part of him – his balancing pole!

The riding figure should be as close as possible to the standing figure, never to the sitting figure...

Elaine looks proud but there is no stiffness or tension in her body. Sitting tall has allowed her weight to fall away and secure her position over the strongest part of the horse – just behind the wither, and over his centre of balance.

For a great halt

Firstly, think how the horse needs energy to move into halt; without energy, he won't be 'through' from behind – so don't push hard with the seat or you will only break off the energy. You will need some in reserve to go forward again!

Instead:

● think 'up and forward' as you ride into halt!
● decide exactly where you want to halt, and believe it will happen;
● at the precise spot, advance your waist towards you hands and think 'resist' or 'fix' (this is a very different feel from 'allowing' through your abdominal muscles as you did for riding forward);
● at the same time, drop and pull your knees a little back to close the legs a little further back – weight in the stirrup!
● the sensation is one of closing down with the seat and leg and quietly fixing the energy of the horse under you;
● almost simultaneously, close the hand around the rein to make a fist; again, resist or 'fix' through the shoulders and elbows – there is no need to pull back;
● the moment the halt is achieved, relax the leg and hand. Sit up, even and neutral.

Afterwards – always reward and reinforce a good result when possible.

Transition – trot to halt

Prior to acting, Lizzie thinks 'halt' at a certain point to balance Prazer and prepare.

Impulsion is arrested by closing the leg just behind the girth and checking gently through the seat, back, elbows and fingers.

The halt is established and squared by slackening off the finger and leg pressure. The rider's weight is central, weight falling away into the stirrups.

Halting

Halting becomes a very subtle sensation, similar to how we stop ourselves on the ground. By thinking 'stop!', our energy concentrates itself somewhere around the solar plexus, then the feeling of halt transfers all the way down and into the horse via the pelvic floor.

The principle of letting our weight down through the centre of the horse is very effective.

Leaning back and thrusting with the seatbones is not the way to halt, since this will prevent the horse from stepping under with the hocks and rounding his back.

On the ground, drawing myself up from a brisk walk into halt makes for a much more effective stop, without losing balance.

If this seems very different to what you've been used to, think logically. How would you stop if you were crossing the road and saw a car? There would be no pushing down – instead, you would draw up. This upward bracing action would allow you to be grounded to the spot without falling out of balance and into the road!

It is exactly the same on horseback. As you draw up, you should feel your weight sink deeper through the pelvic floor, down through the front of stretched, lowered thighs into the stirrups. The stirrups must be aligned under your hips for the weight effect to work. This in turn will gently lock the joints which dampens the energy of the horse. The beauty of doing it this way is that you lighten your weight at the back of the saddle, which allows your horse to step under himself with engaged hindlegs. Too often we see horses halt with hollow, disconnected backs, leaving the hindlegs out behind them.

With subtle weight aids, perfect posture can be maintained. Riding halts and downward transitions in this way allows us to work quietly and with almost invisible aids, using Nature's laws of gravity to bring about the desired response.

Release – immediately!

Remember that no aid is truly effective unless we remember to release the horse the second he gives us a response.

A sensitised horse, like the Lusitanos shown here, will feel the closing down/resisting sensation described above, immediately, and

For great transitions

To help release the horse from incorrect weight aids, we should always try to return to a fairly neutral, centred position. This allows the 'river,' or energy, to flow. To increase or decrease forward movement, it's just a question of opening up or closing down with our own bodies. The legs in turn can either encourage or dampen the flow.

For greater forward activity, we must allow the energy under the bridge or 'through the door' of the pelvis. We can also partially close down to slow, steady or collect, or open more fully to encourage greater stretching, as in extension.

TO OPEN – UPWARD TRANSITION

● **Raise the diaphragm. . . breathe. . . then square and drop the shoulders a little further back than normal;**
● **this bracing action should slide the back seatbones slightly forward to encourage impulsion and energise the horse;**
● **think 'lead' from the waist to encourage the horse to stretch and open up, too;**
● **'allow' through the abs, hips, knees, shoulders, elbows, fingers.**

TO CLOSE – DOWNWARD TRANSITION

● **Sit up but think deeper, especially through the pelvic floor;**
● **feel an all-round contact of the seatbones, including the front;**
● **think 'check', or 'steady' from the waist to encourage the horse to slow or gather himself;**
● **gently 'fix' with the abs, knees, shoulders, elbows and fingers.**

To the onlooker, your position for forward and downward transitions should scarcely alter. The real work is going on somewhere around your midriff and the difference in the rest of the aids should be nuances. However, none of this will work if you are out of balance. If your feet are not aligned under your hips, as in moving on the ground, you will not be effective.

Here, Elaine displays a good central position for dressage.

Her shoulders are nicely squared but not rigid.

Her core tummy and diaphragm muscles support upwards.

The spine straightens at its innermost point where the body flexes gently inward at the loins.

A flat back is not a straight back!

Stiffness in the lower lumbar region. Rounded shoulders. Dropped diaphragm. Lack of abdominal tone.

These aids should be applied evenly. Horses which fall out through the quarters in halt generally do so because the weight aid applied is uneven. If one stirrup is loaded more than the other, the horse will swing into that direction since horses always try to balance themselves under our weight.

We must never forget just how powerful these aids can be, or that the horse must be immediately rewarded when he obeys them.

Opening the door again

Too many riders make the mistake of immediately leaning forward when they wish to move off from a collected gait or halt. This may help the young horse, but with the more experienced horse we risk the probability of dropping him onto the forehand. Raising the diaphragm and squaring the shoulders opens the upper body and helps us to breathe more naturally. The collarbones move into the horizontal as the ribs expand, and this in turn lengthens the rider's spine so that the loins automatically flex forward to support the torso.

It is this natural action of the lower back, often known as yielding or suppling through the loins, which energises the horse to move forward and round up to meet us. The 'allowing' through the back must never be overt. If you think about moving on the ground in good posture, you will realise how little is needed. It's just a matter of thinking forward and your back should automatically yield, and that's it!

A model on the catwalk

There should be no question of rocking or trying to 'move with the horse'. Instead, think of a model gliding down the catwalk – there is no visible sign of her back moving; her shoulders are set back and her upper body elegant. Yet, as with all movement, it's just a matter of letting go a little so that the hips and legs take over. In riding, it's exactly the same. Visualise the energy of the horse passing through you – think 'project!' from back to front, and then ask from the leg. Once this sense of leading forward from the centre is achieved, you can sit more quietly.

The sensation is one of being drawn forward from your waistband by an invisible string. Provided you now support the diaphragm with shoulders squared, the seatbones should quietly engage. From this greater stability, the horse is now able to balance around you. Remember, only when you've made room for your horse in

will halt or decrease speed as required. If the aid continues beyond that point, the horse may even rein back if pressure is still being applied. The moment the correct response is achieved, therefore, we must neutralise the pressures. The legs relax down again, whilst, by sitting up tall again, we soften the abdominal muscles out of 'resist' mode, and think 'allow'.

Everything must remain neutral until the next request. If we go on fussing and re-arranging ourselves, it is hardly surprising if the horse does the same. No wonder so many horses fidget about after they have halted – their riders have forgotten to say "thank you."

These confusions tend to arise when aids are learned parrot-fashion without recognising that applying or releasing pressure constitutes changes of weight. Yet there is nothing new here; my old BHS/Pony Club Manual (1966 edition) reminds us of these often forgotten principles. Under the heading, 'To decrease pace or halt' we read – close both legs, straighten the spine and bring the horse up into a still hand. . . as soon as the horse has obeyed, relax the pressure of the legs and the feeling on the reins'. . . in other words, pressure on, pressure off – it should be so simple.

41

this way should your legs ask him to spring into action. You must always open the door first to release energy, then ask!

Sit tall and proud

Thrusting in the saddle is usually caused by stiffness in the back – the rider tries to compensate for an inability to free up. Sitting proud and tall should not make you stiff; as any physiotherapist will tell you, it should liberate and correct the spine, smoothing out inconsistencies of posture, and allowing the intercostal muscles and discs to do their job and act as shock absorbers.

Collapsing the abdominal muscles forward or leaning backwards flattens the spine out of its natural curves, which in turn may pinch the discs in some places and squeeze them out in others. Elasticity is compromised and damaging pressures are placed on the weakest parts for both horse and human.

Easing your weight off the back

There may be times when you wish to ease your weight forward on your horse's back, particularly on a young, tense or explosive horse. Provided you do this by taking more weight into the knees and stirrups, rather than heavily on the crotch, this can be very encouraging for forward impulsion.

Here again, the only way to do this in balance is to retain the natural flexion of the loins, so once more we need to employ the abdominal muscles to keep us light and supported. Remember, however, all these ideas require subtlety, and everything must work together if we are to keep our horse connected.

Opening the chest and dropping the shoulders back enables Mary to absorb the movement of the horse through a supple back. The energy of the horse can now pass 'through' her seat without loss of balance. This demonstrates the classical ideal of riding 'waist to hands'.

Chapter Four

Impulsion
The role of the legs

In Chapter Three we discussed the idea of using weight momentarily to fix or interrupt movement in our downward transitions. The idea was to think 'resist' or 'close the door' whilst still sitting up and in good posture. We also discussed the sensation of 'allowing' both through the front (abs) and from a supple back, to encourage forward progression. There would be no point in even discussing impulsion until we can understand how fine a line we are treading between channelling energy down and channelling it up a step.

This may come as a surprise to some, since impulsion is often mistaken for speed. But speed on its own is not enough. A horse can run away with us very fast, as though freewheeling out of control, but that is not what is meant by impulsion. Impulsion is more akin to revving the engine and using the gears to distribute power in the way we want. In other words, the horse is under control, engaged and deliberate in his movements. An impulsive horse offers his energy so that we can send him forward in any gait or any mode we wish — collected, extended, forwards, sideways, backwards, upwards, over a jump, and so on – always feeling we have something in reserve. This is impulsion.

But first things first – there can be no impulsion without forwardness, and forwardness itself has little merit unless there is activity, which in the horse means pushing power from behind. Until we can teach the horse to flex and utilise the full range of his hind limb joints as he pushes, there will be no real impulsion.

● **Whilst lightening up through the seat and upper body is fundamental to allowing forward movement to take place –**

● **the key to activating the horse depends on the efficacy of our legs.**

It is no good saying to a rider *"legs on!"* in a riding lesson if, in fact, the legs are acting in a tight, restrictive way and thus impeding or blocking forward movement. Legs which are too far back perch the rider on the fork, with dire results. However, ineffectual, flaccid legs are almost as bad. Ideally, our legs should be light and supple enough to encourage, but toned enough to channel the horse's energy.

The secret to control, therefore, is mobility. Many people are tight through the hip joint simply through lack of exercise. Sedentary lifestyles lead to bad habits, so joints need to be constantly opened and muscles stretched in our day-to-day activities if we are to ride well. It takes time and commitment to tone the muscles just to stay vertical, so for proper aiding it is simply not sufficient to leave things until the next hack out or the next riding lesson. Bad posture on the ground leads to bad posture on horseback and huge misunderstandings between horse and rider.

Stiff or locked hip joints severely restrict the action of the rider's legs and have a spiralling effect on the rest of the joints, often resulting in a stopping aid being given when none was intended. The horse is very sensitive to the feel of our hips in the saddle, but once we train our hips to unblock with exercises on the ground, much greater control over leg position will be attained. We can then make it clear to the horse when we mean to go forward or when we mean to slow down. Many experienced riders I have taught have actually stopped the horse with the leg in every stride. When this is pointed out to them and hips and legs are realigned, they are amazed at the difference in their horse.

Elaine demonstrates just how unbalancing and detrimental to her horse having her legs too far back, can be. This horse feels blocked and hollows, but a younger horse might even rear.

As you think forward, try also to think 'uphill' – the idea is to lighten the horse's shoulders as he moves up a gear. Whilst framing him, make sure the legs don't clamp on and restrict his action.

Mechanics of movement

Nobody walks down the road working out which hip advances, and which leg pushes off to take us forward; it just happens. But it only happens easily because long ago, as toddlers, we learned, through trial and error, the mechanics of movement.

We would be quite unable to advance on the ground if we tipped behind the vertical, as is so often seen in dressage circles, yet the irony is, people are still being taught to ride in this way – the chair seat is very much alive and kicking!

In nature, our legs take us forward because, firstly, we balance over them. After that, it is simply a matter of thinking where to go. Whether we turn right or left, stop, go forward again, step sideways, or even backwards, it presents no problem – we merely think it, and it happens!

Why does it become so much more difficult on horseback? Why can't one simply think what one wants and have the horse immediately respond? Yet it is possible for things to happen this way once we learn to work with nature and become balanced over our feet in the saddle.

Ultimately, the horse will then become so well balanced under us that he merely becomes an extension of our own body. Thus, his legs become our legs, and he can act as we think! Such finesse is very much dependent on our ability to feel the changes of weight and pressures within our own body as we ride.

Forward with energy!

All riders talk about creating impulsion, but since this is a natural phenomenon, it's more a question of creating the conditions to let it happen. Impulsion will grow of its own accord as the horse gets stronger and better balanced in his work. Good posture and good aiding from us will naturally help, and we must be ready to deal with it when it comes.

Having learned in Chapter Three how to 'open

Try it yourself!

Our seat and legs will feel even heavier to the horse if our hips are tight, and the freedom of movement in the leg is severely hampered when the pelvis tips back. If you don't believe me, try it on the ground!

Firstly, mimic the average sitting position, with the waist slightly collapsed and the pelvis slipped back. Try to open one leg outward and away from the hip, without leaning. You will be amazed how difficult it feels.

Now, stand upright, brace the back forward, feel your pelvis move into the vertical, and try again. Suddenly, it all becomes much easier. Your hip joint can now act as nature intended – like a hinge – and once in the saddle you should be able to open both hips so that the legs simply fall into place through gravity alone. This takes all the effort out of bringing your legs around the horse and ensures a much deeper position.

On the ground, Elaine mimics the slightly collapsed upper body position of the average rider.

From this collapsed position Elaine tries to open one leg outward. She immediately loses balance as her leg shoots backward due to locked hip joints. She has very little control over how and where to place her leg.

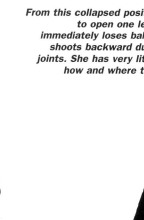

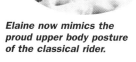

Elaine now mimics the proud upper body posture of the classical rider.

From this proud posture, Elaine now has much greater mobility in her hip joint and is able to open her leg outward in a controlled way, without tilting or losing balance.

Front view: Suzanne has advanced her body close to the pommel; with hips and knees looking forward, this allows her legs to drape around the horse and provide a subtle framework without blocking. The lower leg should hang just free of the horse's side, ready to apply an aid.

Rear view: A correct and unrestricted leg position, where the weight simply falls away from the rider and into the stirrup, is only possible from a balanced upper body position. Note the correct lower back support to help retain a vertical pelvis.

the door' by raising the body's centre of gravity, many people often unwittingly close it again in their desire to push the horse on. They may sit up nicely for walk, but for trot and canter seem unable to believe the horse can advance without a great deal of kicking – all of which involves constant shifts of weight. But is this logical?

How the horse moves in freedom

- Firstly, he engages his hindlegs under him;
- this in turn raises the thoracic spine which 'lightens' the forehand;
- he generally then arches his neck so that the poll is the highest point;
- this liberates his shoulders and forelegs and, propelled from behind, off he goes!

Now let's look at human movement

Imagine a similar scenario where an army sergeant addresses his recruits on the parade ground. He wants them to march off efficiently and with real motivation, so what does he say? *"Look lively! Walk! March!"* And what do they do? They flex their legs under them, brace their backbones, pull their shoulders back, lift their chests and their energy, and off they go. Legs can march for miles once the mechanics are correct. It's the same with horses.

So isn't it illogical to push down with our seat and squeeze the life out of our horse with our legs? Heaving with the bottom merely depresses the horse's spine, and legs which squeeze backward will make him want to move backward. This does have its uses, as we shall see later on, but not for better impulsion!

For great forward movement

People talk about a well trained horse moving 'off the leg'. This is a good expression since 'on-off' with the leg is a much better way of asking for impulsion than 'on-on-on'! Moving up a gear from walk to trot, from a collected trot to a more ground-covering one, or collected to medium canter etc, will work better when the signals are clear, short and sweet...

● Firstly, think up and straighten the spine with the shoulders back;
● feel your lower back flex forward to support your hips in the saddle centre;
● make both legs as 'long' as possible, thighs and knees in contact, lower leg 'hanging' close, but just away from the horse's sides;
● think 'forward!' and make a quick, deliberate 'nip' or 'close together' with the inner flat part of the lower leg at the girth;
● visualise what you want! Actually see your leg create more 'spurt' as the channel of energy is momentarily narrowed;
● immediately release the pressure and allow your leg to return to the hanging position so the horse can pass freely forward and 'through' your aids;
● closing the lower leg should not affect the thigh position; use the knee as a hinge to open and close the lower leg;
● if nothing happens, 'nip' again, a little more smartly – then release;
● if a third 'nip' is required, tap the horse with a long dressage stick just behind the calf – as with the legs – just one 'on-off!'

Always be quick to reward when your horse has understood; don't punish him by asking for too much, too soon... better to have a moment's rest and start again. This way he will want to offer more!

In all forward movement, there must be an allowing feel through your back and waist whilst the shoulders remain down and back. Once in motion, try to feel your allowing upper body keeping your horse going. After that, the legs merely keep rhythm, lightly brushing the horse's side as he builds up momentum, and no more.

Once the rider's hips are upright and central, the stirrup leather should hang down vertically. This allows the weight of the leg to fall down, unconstricted and into the stirrup in a fairly neutral balance. Leg at the girth generally denotes toe level with the girth.

What can go wrong?

● If the rider fails to sit up, he/she may block the horse before he has even started; be careful always to take off the 'handbrake' before you apply the leg!

● Too many riders use the leg in a backward direction, and this may make the horse want to go backward (see the aids for rein-back).

● If the aid is given as a prolonged squeeze, the pressure may stifle the horse's desire to move forward.

● If the rider continually uses the legs once the horse is going forward, the aid becomes less and less effective. Too much leg will eventually deaden the horse's sides and he will no longer want to listen for the aids.

Never forget that every horse is different. While some will require scarcely any leg at all, others may need a firmer close. Whilst the intensity of the aid may differ, the manner and place in which it is given should be similar, as this acts on the horse's natural instincts.

Flexibility of the hip joints is very important in riding. Good posture on the ground and the classical riding seat has allowed me to remain supple in the hip, even in my fourth decade of riding. Don't practise this at home unless you, too, are fit and flexible.

Refining the leg aids

Once riders become aware that every time they close the legs they are making a change of weight or pressure on the horse's back via their seat or pelvis as well as on his sides, they learn to refine their aids. Gradually, the legs take on a light 'breathing' quality so that the horse can operate in relative freedom. Horses become much more impulsive once we release them from constriction, and particularly once we know just where to stimulate them.

Find the sensitive spot

The trick is to motivate the horse by acting on a ticklish or sensitive spot. The reflex system can produce a chain of reaction which will reverberate around the rest of his body. That is why a discerning leg will not only stimulate good forward impulsion but sustain it in an apparently effortless way.

The old masters taught that the rider's leg, acting at the girth, would 'lighten' the horse. Science tells us that offshoots of the intercostal nerve are clustered around this point, which in turn work on the horse's dorsal and abdominal muscles. Light stimulation here will help free the shoulder and the thoracic lumbar spine, which comprises the entire forehand. The leg at the girth also supports the horse's forehand. On a circle, for example, the rider's inside hip should move forward to complement the support of the inside leg and encourage the horse to bend into it.

Toned, not tight

It is important to remind riders that light legs are never sloppy legs! Letting your knees and thighs gape open throws out the wrong signals and gives the horse an escape route. For example, on a circle, if the outside knee and thigh are very slack, the horse may well fall out through his outside shoulder. Similarly, if the inside thigh does not support, he will drift in. Think of your thighs as an extension of your seat so the horse is quietly contained within the correct channel.

For this reason, our legs should always be toned, but never tight. Tone comes from learning to stretch and lengthen the muscles fibres of both the thigh and calf so that the legs remain supple, but in place.

Think of quietly framing the horse through the seat, leg and rein. On this right circle we see the importance of the rider's inside hip supported forward to promote the correct bend.

How to stretch your legs

Gently push your knees downward and away from the pelvis, letting your weight flow downwards and into the stirrup. This is especially helpful for riders who have a tendency to grip upward and tense the calf muscles. Try simply to think of the stirrup as a foot-rest – something to spring off – whilst allowing gravity to do its job.

Changing old habits

If you are a rider with 'busy legs' you may have to school yourself to resist the temptation to aid at every stride. Never wear spurs until you are sure you know how to 'let go' with the leg. The 'off' should start to become more prolonged than the 'on'. Most horses work better without

spurs, but if you feel the need, your use of the spur must be as controlled and as light as the use of the leg.

In teaching your horse to offer more impulsion, be content with a little improvement at a time, and reward frequently. Allow him to stretch after just a few good forward (not rushing) strides. Gradually, this can be built up to a few circuits, and so on.

You won't get impulsion by going on and on in the same rhythm, same gait, same, boring old sequence. Constant transitions and changes of direction do far more for impulsion, as does learning to reduce the intensity of the lower leg aid. This way, your horse will want to offer more until the less visible the signal, the more he will move 'off' your leg.

Dampening impulsion

In halt and rein-back, the message is changed. It's at this point that tight or blocking riders may find they are getting halt and rein-back when they don't necessarily want it!

When pupils new to my schoolmaster horses sit on them for the first time, it's interesting to see the horses' reactions. If their legs hang long, toned but relaxed, they will go forward nicely. However, with riders who are tight in the hip and tense in the leg, they have been known to hold back in every stride, and even move into piaffe, or rein-back. It all depends how and where they feel the leg. So, what are the main differences?

Forward and back – in a nutshell

● **The feel in the leg asking for forward impulsion should be light, swift and, if necessary, sharp. The aid is applied close to the girth.**
● **The feel in the leg asking for slow down, halt or rein back, is a steady, dampening down sensation. The aid is applied a little behind the girth.**
When people ask why these aids work so successfully and seem surprised that there is no question of pulling the horse's head in for rein-back, I explain that all the horse is doing is moving under the rider's weight, so the horse merely follows. The moment the rider sits up again and allows the leg to swing into its original 'hanging' vertical place, toe quietly aligned at the girth, the horse is released. Forward and onward again!

For a great rein-back

● Sit tall, lighten the weight at the back of the saddle by sitting more into the thighs, the knee well under you;

● now close both lower legs gently against the horse about a hand's breadth behind the girth;

● at the same time, visualise a dam lowering and the banks closing in around your river of energy, so the forward exit is closed;

● as you feel your horse respond – he should ease his weight onto his hocks – release the pressure, then ask again;

● an on-off signal from the leg in the correct place should now elicit a step backward as the horse merely follows the weight of the leg back;

● repeat the sequence for each step you take.

For rein-back simply sit tall, alleviate weight from the back of the saddle by deepening the knees, then 'ask' with the leg so the horse can step back in diagonal pairs.

51

What can go wrong?

● A young, sensitive horse, learning rein-back for the first time, can easily panic; it's important to teach him to move back in the stable from your hand before trying in the saddle.

● Fast, whizzy horses can panic too – most people are much too strong with the legs so the horse can block, hollow, or even rear – which is why you must be very gentle with both seat and leg, and reassure at every stage.

● So you've been careful, but your horse seems to rush and lose balance. You may have forgotten the 'on-off' use of the leg. Ask and release with each diagonal step taken, and always neutralise your seat and leg each time the horse responds.

● If your horse is crooked in the rein-back this is generally caused by unevenness in the rider's seat or leg pressure. The horse will move away from your stronger leg. Even yourself up, then ride the exercise against the arena wall, with the horse slightly bent to the inside. This should correct the deviation of the quarters.

● If your horse simply seems not to recognise the aid – what then? This is often because there is no difference in the rider's seat. If your hip joints are locked, or you always ride with legs too far back, the horse cannot recognise the new aid.

● What if you simply can't get the 'feel' and are not sure whether you're doing it right or wrong? Try walking backwards on the ground with a nice, tall posture. That will give you the feel you are looking for, especially in your pelvis.

This is a reasonably good rein-back showing the legs moving back in diagonal pairs. However, too much leg can cause the horse to drop the contact – which in a less schooled horse could cause real problems such as running backwards. This all goes to show how subtle we must be.

Chapter Five

In the stirrups - straightness, turns and circles

To use the stirrups correctly, most riders will benefit from work without them! This may sound like a contradiction, but it is not. The real purpose of the stirrups is not to keep us on board – our seat and thighs are supposed to do that – rather they are there to help us balance and rebalance so we can change our weight in the saddle, as well as alleviate the horse's back from unwanted pressure. To improve the seat, therefore, lunge lessons without stirrups to centralise and deepen our position is a vital part of training. Once riders are secure in themselves, they can then learn to use the stirrups more appropriately.

It was that great master or 'father of equitation', Sieur de la Guérinière who wrote in 1735 *"... the aid of putting weight into the stirrups is the subtlest of all the aids..."* Not only did they serve as *"counterweights to straighten the haunches and to hold the horse straight"*, they could also, as he went on to explain, be used to turn, circle and move sideways.

Most riders know that the aids to turn are inside leg on the girth, outside leg behind the girth. But how many people interpret this in terms of feel and weight adjustment in the stirrups which have such a huge bearing on the horse? Too often, people give the leg aid but then resort to very strong rein aids because their horse has failed to respond. The worst scenario is when you see a rider dragging their horse round by the head and neck so that the hindlegs spin out into the next county!

Lead with your weight

We have already spoken of sitting fractionally deeper into one seatbone or the other to encourage the horse to turn, come around or move under our weight. There is nothing new

about downward pressure bringing the horse towards you – remember the sack simile? Basically, the horse will always try to step under the increased load, provided there's room to manoeuvre!

Correct! Deepening into the inside stirrup helps the rider stay central: it helps the horse bend through circles, turns, or simply staying out to the track. Note the vertical leather.

Keep it subtle

To achieve an immediate response from the horse, the main structure needs to be as stable and central as possible. No weight aid will work if everything else is 'out of sync'. Neither will any aid work effectively in isolation; in every action we make there is always the need to counterbalance. Remember, these aids are all about subtle adjustments, translated to the horse as 'feel'.

Incorrect! Deepening through bracing pushes the rider back and hardens the leg against the horse. This will discourage bend and annoy the horse. Note the position of the leather, in front of the vertical.

Crude weight aids will only confuse the horse and even achieve the opposite effect of what is desired. For example, when you're asked to place a little more weight into the inside stirrup for bend, it is counter-productive to push against the iron as this will stiffen your leg and possibly push the horse the other way. Deepening the inside leg should not involve bracing it. Think of it as an invitation to the horse, never a block.

You and your legs

In riding circles, corners or turns, your legs have two different roles. The inside leg acts on the forehand and should support, stimulate or invite at the girth. The job of the outside leg, placed a little behind the girth and acting on the quarters, is more complex. Basically, it may be used to allow, support, encourage or activate more from behind, indicate sideways, or initiate turning.

A lack of understanding about these different roles will result in leg aids which may hinder rather than help the horse. If the rider hasn't first freed up both legs by sitting centrally, quiet, tall and upright (thus enabling the hip joints to open) the weight aids will not be felt. In fact, they may throw out conflicting messages. And, since every aid we give involves changing or displacing our weight, they need to be very clear. So think of your horse and try to imagine exactly what he needs to feel from you.

Moving out...

In staying out to the track, or moving your horse into a bigger circle, think of working him from the inside out...
● Let your inside leg act in a supporting *against* way, with the leg touching lightly at the girth to send the horse forward and outward.
● Let your outside leg continue to support, but sometimes placing a little more weight into the outside stirrup may help keep him out.

Moving in...

In turning off the track, or bringing your horse into a smaller circle, think of working him from the outside in...
● Your inside leg act must maintain forwardness, but in a pressing *downward* way, with the stirrup just free of the horse's body to allow him to move into or around it.
● Let your outside leg act in a pressing *against* his body way, so he moves away from it.

In the manège, think of turning onto the track as part of a circle. When we leave it, the feeling is more akin to riding part of a square, although in both cases we want to encourage bend. While most people have no trouble with the *against* feel of the leg, many people have difficulty with the downward feel. This is generally caused by tension, so let us look at some pointers to help both bend and turn at the same time.

Left: *If the horse is reluctant to move out in the circle, try placing a little more pressure in the outside stirrup, whilst retaining inside bend.*

The rider has allowed her weight to sink correctly into her left inside stirrup without bracing, so the horse is invited to bend and move into it.

For a great turn ...
(Away from the track on the right rein)

● Feel gently on the inside (right) opening rein for flexion – but without pulling back;
● advance your inside hip and let your inside leg 'drop down' so the toe aligns with the girth (just visible);
● allow your weight to fall away – you should keep pressure in the bar of the inside stirrup, but no sense of pushing against it;
● feel your inside seat bone deepen in sympathy;
● open the outside (left) hip to free the outside leg further back;
● apply more active pressure behind the girth and close with the outside leg to turn the main body of the horse away;
● close your outside rein towards or against the base of the horse's neck to guide the forehand away;
● as your horse turns 'in one piece' your whole upper body turns with him in one piece. Never turn more than your horse!

Straightness

Having turned, one of the hardest things is to ride forward straight again. So many lurch onto the inside shoulder after the turn. This is often caused by part of the general 'frame' of the rider's seat and upper leg giving way. For this reason, it's important that the rider's thighs remain toned to support the horse in the turn otherwise – in a change of rein for example – the horse will be lurching from one side to the other, as he goes off in the opposite direction.

Having discussed the various changes of weight for moving in and out, turning etc, we should now appreciate that to ride straight will also require a feeling of neutrality. Our lower legs should hang in roughly equal balance to ensure even pressure in each stirrup iron. This requires a very balanced upper body position with open hips and toned, stretched legs, which have learned to 'let go' except when making a specific request.

We have already discussed the dangers of bracing the leg artificially against the stirrup; instead, we must allow gravity to do the work for us so that our weight is plumb*. After all, we don't consciously push with the heel when we walk (yet it strikes the ground ahead of the toe); so it should be no different when riding. Gravity allows our foot to remain in the stirrup and the feeling is more adhesive than grinding downward.

Francois Baucher, a 19th Century French riding master, described the sensation of using the stirrups correctly as *"riding in bedroom slippers"* - the slipper providing a comfortable footrest. Once you think this way, and the horse feels your legs drop around him easily by virtue of their own weight and not through any muscular tension, it is much easier for him to straighten out. Of course, we may than have to make tiny adjustments to keep him straight, but at least he will be free of conflicting pressures when we don't mean it.

In the balance

To consolidate all this, it is helpful to think of the rider's body as the main support in a pair of scales. Think of the stirrups as being the extremities of the scales or, if you go for bareback riding, think of the

Lizzie prepares to change the rein from right to left as she crosses the short diagonal. Gently transferring pressure into the left stirrup will help Prazer into the new bend that follows.

seat bones. Good riders think of both. For all forward and straight riding, your 'long' legs and seatbones are in roughly equal balance. When you wish to change things, the adjustment of pressure into the stirrup (or seatbone) on the side you wish to move towards, should be minuscule. Adding or removing the smallest weight can change the balance on a pair of scales, and so it is in riding.

Remember also that the seat and upper body should remain quiet. Too much seat, too much wobble in the rider's torso, creates conflicting messages and will confuse the horse. He can only tune into our aids if the messages are simple and clear, and this means getting rid of background 'noise'. So think quiet and vertical before you act!

Reading your mind

We often hear riders say; *"I just thought it – and my horse did it!"* The truth is, they looked between the horse's ears, thought of what they wanted, and natural balance took over. One of the wonderful things about horses is that they always try to 'pick us up' again whenever they

feel we are out of balance. We can gently capitalise on this when riding movements, by inviting the horse to go where we want, such as half-pass, shoulder-in, etc.

Simple changes of direction can be executed with minimum fuss and far less reliance on the rein. We think right, our weight goes quietly right, the horse moves right. Of course, it is possible to make horses turn by simply leaning inwards. In full flight on a racecourse this is exactly what a practised jockey will do. As the horse hugs the rail, the jockey tilts to the inside of the curve and the horse comes with him. It is the speed and centrifugal force involved that keeps them from falling over.

In dressage, these tactics are much frowned upon and will not necessarily work. Why? Firstly, we like to feel our horse balanced, upright and in control; secondly, we are not moving at great speed so are less helped by gravitational forces; thirdly, there are many transitions as well as tight corners and figures to negotiate, so to cope accurately and safely, we will need to introduce an element of bend.

Teaching the horse to bend

A horse does not learn to bend overnight since several muscle systems are involved. In very simple terms, muscles work in pairs and will only work harmoniously when one set stretches as the other flexes. With a stiff horse, this may involve hours of slow and careful bend and stretch exercises.

How else can we help this natural process?
● As you 'ask' with the inside rein for bend, the outside rein must sufficiently allow.
● As you 'ask' with the inside leg at the girth, the outside leg should move back to encourage stretch.
● As you straighten again, make sure everything returns to normal. Equalise!

On a circle, the horse will need to stretch as much to the outside as he bends to the inside. It is this bending which will allow him to hold the circumference of the circle without falling in or out. The smaller the circle, the more supple the horse needs to be. This is particularly relevant in canter, and it's not unusual to see horses fall in when cantering because they have been expected to cope with tight circles before they are sufficiently supple. However, all this can be remedied with correct schooling and knowing which aids to employ.

Above: Moving out into a 10m canter circle requires a supple outside hip to allow the horse to stretch to the outside as he bends around the inside leg.
Below: Closing the circle needs more pressure against the horse from the outside leg and rein. while the inside (just visible) stirrup and seatbone will be gently weighted.

For a great circle
(at any gait)
● Lead the horse off the track in the manner described for 'moving in' with fractionally more pressure in the inside stirrup.
● Establish the size of the circle with which your horse will easily cope – 20 metres for a young or novice horse, 15-10 metres for the more mature horse.
● Gently ask your horse to flex from the poll through a soft, asking inside rein. You should just see the shimmer of the inside eye and rim of the nostril, no more!
● Think of your outside rein allowing enough for the horse to stretch into the bend, but retaining enough to control the bend and to keep him on the same circle.
● Your inside leg should be long and softly active at the girth to give impulsion, bend and support to the forehand – a feel of inside-leg-to-outside-hand may help.
● With your outside leg further back, think of smoothing the progress of the quarters along, aiding the hindlegs to step under rather than falling out.
● At the furthest point of the circle, think a little more into your inside seatbone as you direct the horse from the outside back in to your starting point.
● Look between the horse's ears and never turn more than your horse. Stay upright and square to axis – the more central your body, the better your feel for the balance of the horse.

Biomechanics of circles
To ride a circle correctly, it helps to understand what bending actually involves for the horse. To supple or soften to the inside, the horse must take a deeper step underneath himself with the inside hind leg. This involves rotating and lowering the inside haunch, which requires greater flexing or bending of all the hind limb joints; hip, stifle, hock and fetlock. This permits him to yield his body into the shape of the figure

requested without tilting or falling over. But it will only come about successfully with correct aiding – one of the most important influences being that of the rider's hips. We should always slightly lead with the inside hip in the turn or circle in the same way as we would for walking a turn or a circle on the ground.

The correct alignment of the hips is;
● inside hip forward – to support the rider's inside leg position at the girth;
● outside hip slightly back – to promote the necessary freeing up of the rider's outside leg to act on the quarters.

What can go wrong?
Circle getting smaller than you want
● incorrect or too much bend;
● too much weight in the inside stirrup;
● tilting in or collapsing through the waist (most common);
● too much opening of the inside rein;

● outside hand shooting forward – horse no longer retained on his circle;
● rider's inside leg weak and ineffectual – unable to give support. Gaping knee and thigh increasing the weight load inward;
● outside leg too strong;
    As you can see, the reasons are many and varied, but what is certain is that if one tiny part of you is out of balance, it can easily throw everything out of balance!

Circle getting bigger than you want
● incorrect or lack of bend;
● rider tilting or collapsing onto outside seatbone;
● too much 'take' with the inside rein – horse jackknifes onto outside shoulder;
● insufficient 'give' with the outside rein;
● too much inside leg – particularly if used too far back;
● weak, untoned outside leg – gaping knee and

Wrong! Too many riders pull back on the rein to turn or decrease the circle. This creates a twist in the rider's upper body which blocks the horse to the inside and throws the rider's weight to the outside.

thigh, increasing weight load to outside;
● losing the support of inside hip, upper body overturning in circle.

Another fault common to both the above problems is when the rider simply forgets to turn with the horse. Depending on your other aids, this can either push the horse further out, or allow him to fall in.

General flexion

Never forget the fact that the horse is broader across the quarters than at the shoulders. For that reason we should always be conscious of a very gentle flexion to the inside whether riding along the track, moving out or moving in. This is obtained by a very slight give and take on the inside rein to ask for bend through the poll and a softening of the horse's jaw.

A poor head position, or tension in the rider's jaw can transfer itself to the horse very easily. We should try to ride with the crown of the head forming the highest point, whilst the neck just touches our collar. Pretend you too have a poll – roughly where the knobble at the top of your hat is situated – and think of flexing there, like the horse, by gently dropping your chin. Always look through his ears, so if you are asking him to flex right or left, there should be very slight turning that way with your own head position.

Never tilt your head! Instead, it's the dropping of the chin and relaxation of the jaw which allows you to glance into the direction of travel so the horse can mirror you. Whether it's a corner, turn, a big or small circle, you should just be able to see your horse's eye and rim of his nostril at all times. However, it's no good acting on the horse's neck alone. Correct flexion must, of course, be attained through the entire body of the horse. Therefore, once the hands and upper body have gently indicated, the legs should gradually take over so that the inside rein contact can be softened.

Around the girth area is the optimum place for bend and it is up to the rider continually to encourage this yielding to the inside, if the horse is not to fall in or out through the shoulders – a sure sign of stiffness. However, too much bend is almost as bad as no bend at all. Remember that, having allowed with the outside rein for stretch, the same rein will need gently to check and support when the horse has turned sufficiently.

Remember, whether we are talking about the upper body, head, the seat, the hands or our

legs, every step that we take in riding involves the subtle use of our weight. It's just a question of saying to your horse *"Here's where I am! Follow me! Come and share my space...!"* However, only by providing clear boundaries can we show him where to find that space!

Thinking left automatically allows the rider's body to act left; the inside hip leads and supports the bend, with the yielding of the horse reflected throughout.

* The plumbline theory is thoroughly explained in *The Classical Seat.*

Chapter Six

In the stirrups
- a good basic canter

Using the stirrups appropriately can make all the difference in the world to the canter and canter changes, but how many riders appreciate the importance of these subtle weight aids to achieve a clear strike off and a good balanced canter from day one? Ask the average rider to lead off on a given leg in canter from the centre line of the manège and few will sound very confident about offering it. Wisely, most people will prefer to start cantering out of a circle or corner, to ensure the correct lead, and only then proceed to riding straight lines. They often prefer to finish on a corner too, otherwise we often see the horse shoot from under them in a downward transition. For many, therefore, the whole process of cantering on the 'correct' leg can be a somewhat hit-or-miss affair. How can we improve things?

The raison d'être

First, it is important to understand the logic behind the traditional canter aids – ie, inside leg at the girth, outside leg behind the girth. Most riders know that the canter starts with the horse's outside hindleg, so the action of the rider's outside leg seems justified. But why does this aid alone not always work? And why in canter right, for example, does the right leg on the girth not always seem sufficient?

Indeed, without understanding what the 'feel' of the aids indicates to the horse, how can we even be sure that we are asking in the correct way? Wouldn't it be comforting to know that we can ask for canter at any time, in any given situation, on a straight line, on the opposite rein to which we are working, on a particular leg out on a hack to make a change for the horse, etc, and to be so sure of the feel and the reasons why, that we never get the wrong lead again?

Who to blame?

The first thing we need to do is be humble. I have come across horses that have a strong preference to canter on the same leg all the time, no matter in which direction they are going, and the rider is convinced there is something wrong with their horse. Very occasionally this may be so, but rarely. I have also been told by many riders that their horse likes to 'play' up by offering the opposite lead to that which was asked for. In both cases, students are often astounded when I tell them that it's not the horse who has misunderstood them, but rather the other way round!

All this goes to show that it's not enough just to know the aids parrot-fashion. To be good riders and produce fail-safe results, we need to appreciate what the horse needs to feel from us in order to understand. As with the previous chapters, we must underpin our work by thinking in terms of pressure and balance in every aid

In the upward phase of canter, the inside leg, acting lightly at the girth, helps give lift and impetus to the forehand.

Although forward, the canter looks a little flatter as the rider's inside leg drifts back.

that we give, and recognise that of all the gaits, the canter will be the most affected when we get things wrong. Why? Because both in the moment of suspension and in other moments when the horse only has one foot on the ground, the balance can be precarious. So, purely from the aspect of self-preservation, he may have to compensate for our incorrect balance by doing the opposite to what we thought we asked.

Let me now impress the importance of the feeling behind the giving of the traditional canter aids – inside leg at the girth: outside leg behind. By necessity, the pressures involved should feel totally different from each other. We have already discussed the need not to trap the horse in the middle of two opposing forces, so it's important that as one aid asks or demands, the other should receive, support or allow. This rule applies more than ever in the canter so that both sets of aids can complement and not oppose each other.

A fail-safe method for the correct lead should be when the rider learns to 'lead' with their own body in addition to simply asking the horse to push off from behind. The horse will naturally be inclined to canter right when he feels our centre of gravity indicate right. We do this by keeping our inside hip forward, gently stepping into our right stirrup to make way for the right fore, and by slightly weighting the inside seat bone. However, there is far more to it than that, as we shall discover. Firstly, we must learn to free up like the horse. Secondly, our upper body must remain very balanced and we must be careful not to twist; too much feel on the inside rein can cause this. Instead, think of easing the inside rein in the canter depart and

Here, the lack of inside leg support leads to a very unbalanced turn out of the corner - a common sight.

In canter, the outside aids are as important, in their way, as those of the inside. The outside leg must allow and support, as well as activate the hindquarters.

straightening the horse's neck with the outside rein. This will help free the horse's inside shoulder.

In the case of the outside leg in its asking role, we must make sure our outside hip opens or unlocks sufficiently to free the whole leg back. This will allow the horse to stretch to the outside as he naturally bends around your inside leading leg (see Chapter Five). But even before we go through the leg and body aids, one by one, it's important to include one other vital ingredient (which is often forgotten) in the initial strike off.

Think uphill!

Many riders are so keen to hurry forward and onward, they completely forget that canter is a wonderfully uphill, springy gait, and that in the moment of total suspension when all four hooves are off the ground, any interference will upset the balance. Most horses will avoid disaster by 'falling' back to trot. Others, more eager, simply get stronger in the hand as they are driven onto the forehand. Try, therefore, to

use your long tummy muscles and sit tall, not only for the upward transition, but also during the moment of suspension and again, for that downhill phase of the canter when the balance can be so threatening for the horse. Unless the rider stays quiet, central and supportive, it will be very difficult for the horse to engage his hocks either for the desired strike off, or to continue forward in balance. That is why so many horses either carry on the wrong leg, become disunited or simply 'run away' from their riders in trot. Why, exactly, does this happen?

The most common mistake

Problems normally arise when we brace with the back of the thigh and calf and push against the stirrup, rather than stepping down into it. This can cause a debilitating spiral effect;

● the stirrup (and pressure) moves forward ahead of the rider's seat, with the toe aligning itself around the horse's elbow;

● this may block the horse's inside shoulder and push him onto the opposite lead for strike off;

● losing the alignment of inside hip-inside heel

Right: To remain in canter, don't push against the horse with the inside leg, as shown here.

Sit centrally and allow your weight to flow down into a supportive inside stirrup so you can lead your horse forward without interruption.

allows the rider's inside seatbone to slide back;
● this hampers the engaging inside hind on which the horse needs to balance, so he may go disunited, or simply refuse to canter;
● the rider tries to rectify these problems by overturning the upper body to the inside;
● this only compounds the problems above.

What the rider needs to do is look straight through the horse's ears, square up, realign the feet under (not ahead) of the hips and start again!

In addition, no horse – however well balanced – likes the feel of remaining unsupported on a corner or circle, which is where more people ask for canter. This is where the feel of the inside leg, acting correctly at the girth, is so vital – not just to initiate the transition, but to provide something for him to balance around. Simply remind yourself of the aids for bend, place more pressure on the ball of the foot, and then ask for canter in the normal way.

Remember, the act of stepping into the inside stirrup in the canter depart will alleviate weight from the back of the saddle. This makes room for the hindlegs to engage so that the horse springs, rather than falls, into canter. Top level riders call this 'lightening' the seat. Once that first step of canter is taken, your inside leg may have to support more against the horse to increase impulsion and maintain bend, but there should always be that sense of weight down, rather than too much pressure against. If the downward pressure is suddenly removed, don't blame the horse if he thinks you want to return to trot!

Pushing the horse into canter by leaning back and coming down hard with the seatbones may, if you're lucky, achieve a transition to canter. But in the logical scheme of things, such action is much more likely to push the horse into a faster and flatter trot. It certainly won't ensure you get the correct strike off.

For great canter transitions

A nice, soft upward transition with a light seat, taking the weight slightly forward.

● Keep the upper body square to axis and avoid any twisting, even on a circle.
● Lighten the seat at the back of the saddle.
● Sit a little deeper into the inside seatbone, keeping the knee well down.
● Touch the horse lightly at the girth with the inside leg.
● Then, deepen the inside stirrup, just away from his side.
● Open the outside hip joint.
● Draw the outside leg back and clearly nudge the horse from behind into canter.

To remain in canter, don't go on 'asking' with the inside leg. You may wish to give more active support for bend, impulsion and staying out to the track, but it must not depart from its place. Remember too, weighting the inside stirrup is an aid in itself and the average horse is more likely to stay in canter when he's given the freedom to do so. So, if you feel the canter 'dying' use more outside leg and try to keep the inside leg under you.

A good way to freshen up the canter is to adopt the forward seat by balancing your weight in both stirrups and ride some free, forward medium strides along the long side of the arena. Horses generally love doing this and it's a good way to work on transitions within the gait when the horse is ready – long sides in big canter; short sides in normal canter. You can do the same out hacking, especially when cantering up slopes and hills.

Sitting deep in medium canter may well restrict the gait and cause hollowing if practised too early in the horse's education. Use a light seat to encourage the horse to really use his back and reserve sitting until roughly elementary dressage level, when the horse should be more muscled due to better engagement behind.

Allow your horse's back to round and free up by riding medium canter in the stirrups along the long side of the arena.

Downward transitions

Downward transitions are much easier than one might imagine. Most people do too much when they bring the horse from canter to trot. Again, pushing against the horse may make him hollow, or 'peck' onto the forehand. Basically, we want his back to remain up and round in the downward transitions, as well as in the upward ones, so it's important not to use the seat harshly or to block the engagement of the hocks. Only by easing his own weight back on the quarters can the horse pick himself up easily and without loss of balance. So help him do this, not by squashing him, rather by sitting up and making room!

Remember always, less is more, so if you think how often in the past your horse has fallen out of canter before you asked, you probably have the answer! The truth is you probably did ask, without meaning to, only you did not recognise this as having been a request. What do I mean by this?

Generally, good riders think about maintaining the canter transition position of their hips and legs throughout the canter. In other words, they keep the inside leg lightly at the girth, outside leg behind it, all the time they are cantering. This does not mean that they keep asking and asking. They simply support and mirror the horse in the canter position which keeps the correct balance. It also means that their legs are always at the ready to reinforce the aid when necessary. The only time they move their legs back into a bilateral 'normal' position is when they want to return to walk or trot. At this point, they simply sit up, gently resist through the fingers and upper body, and allow the legs to hang equally again. In this way, the horse can answer their request with minimum fuss and ease of movement.

From this you may deduce that producing a good canter is not always to do with more, more, more. It's much more to do with initiating greater feel and sometimes doing rather less that you might normally. Of all the gaits, canter is the most airborne, so it's very much a question of knowing when and where to act, and when and where to let go and free up. This is one of the greatest lessons in horsemanship.

A nice soft downward transition from canter to walk. Think up through the diaphragm and allow the inside leg to drop back again.

Developing sensitivity in your legs

'Letting our weight down' is much more to do with allowing than doing. To develop the sensitivity to allow your weight down, take both legs out of the stirrups whilst the horse is stationary and just let them hang without support so that gravity can do its work. You should find that this lowers your knees without having to force them, so that the muscles of the thighs and calves feel relatively relaxed. Simply think of making your legs a little longer than usual. Next, try to keep the same feeling in your mind and quietly retake the stirrups. You may well wish to put them down a hole, but don't over-do this! If you can keep your legs long but stable in this way, with the toe aligned roughly with the girth, you should be much closer to using your weight as nature intended.

Practise on the ground

Cantering for the horse is much akin to skipping for us, so it's useful to practise things on the ground to get the feel of what we should be doing.

In canter left we will only skip off correctly to lead on the left leg, for example, if the right leg is drawn back to push off. This involves keeping the inside, left hip looking forward while the outside right hip opens. Many people lock the outside hip, and this may prevent the horse engaging through with the outside hind in his canter depart. A good test of opening your outside hip is when, on the ground, you can stay in balance with your outside leg on the same track as the lead leg.

Be the horse!

To enhance your feel of canter, stretch tall and skip as though you were the horse! Note that in order to 'canter' left in good balance, my left hip leads while my right leg pushes.

If your outside hip is nicely supple, your horse should never again mistake the strike off aid, provided you slightly weight the inside leading seatbone and stirrup at all times.

First phase, strike off!

Second phase, lead established.

In all phases of the canter, support with the inside hip and try to think 'up and forward' just as you would when skipping on the ground.

Chapter Seven

Lateral movements – moving away from the inside leg

In Chapter Five we discussed the effects of accentuating the feeling of pressure into one or the other stirrup to bring about an effect. This transmits a weight aid to the horse by gently increasing the load on one side of the 'pair of scales' represented by our body and our legs.

Since comfort demands that horses constantly try to come under our weight to 'pick us up', we can soon educate them to listen for these small adjustments to help move them more into the desired direction. This is very noticeable in the showjumping arena, particularly where quick changes of rein and balance are constantly required.

By the same token, we should now appreciate that normal forward progression requires a fairly neutral seat. We must ensure that our legs hang as quietly and as evenly as possible to ensure that the pressure in the stirrups is more or less equal – except when we want to change things.

Balance and counterbalance

For work in the manège there will, sadly, be few occasions when the horse will be ridden dead straight. Coming up the centre line or riding the diagonal are obvious examples, but most of the time, with constant corners and turns, our

Here, in collected trot, my inside leg asks Espada to soften and bend as my inside hip leads him into the right circle.

Weight down! weight against!

Basically, these aids are not difficult.

We have seen how downward pressure weighting the seatbone/stirrup (on the same side) invites more inward movement as in turning, decreasing the circle, stepping more under, etc.

We have also seen how pressure against – by nudging or pressing the leg (knee and thigh may be included) on the same side, invites more outward movement, enlarging the circle, moving sideways, etc.

EVEN MORE IMPORTANT is to use a combination of both!

As one of these actions works the inside of the horse's body, the other action may work the outside, and vice versa, but not always – it all depends what you want. Sometimes, the same leg may be doing two different jobs or 'feels', virtually at the same time. So, remember our maxim – never trap the horse between the aids, always give him a little space to offer his response. The main thing is to recognise what you are doing and to feel for the correct aid.

ALSO, in between these actions, always neutralise your aids to feel and give the horse time to carry out your request.

weight or turning aids will prove invaluable.

We have already discussed the importance of inside bend and how this is achieved by deepening the inside stirrup or seatbone, whilst the outside leg encourages more longitudinal stretch. Most horses will also benefit from some positive inside leg support as well, especially where they are stiff and have a tendency to 'fall in'. So, in addition to the idea of 'weight down', or increased pressure to the inside, we have touched upon the idea of increased pressure acting against the body of the horse around the girth area.

This is generally described as 'inside leg to outside hand' or, in my terminology, 'weight against' and is particularly relevant when working on the horse's stiffer side. The feeling

should be rather like moulding plasticine; your lower leg moulds and massages with gentle pressure aids against the horse's ribcage until you feel him yield his body into the shape of the circle or figure being ridden. You can give added support as necessary with the knee and thigh.

Experienced riders are generally familiar with this concept, many discovering it for themselves without ever being instructed to do so. What they don't always recognise is that the inside (weight against) principle may prove too much when working the horse on the opposite rein. If the horse is very bendy or hollow the other way, the rider will need to relax the pressure of the inside leg on that side, and to think more of riding from the outside leg into the figure being ridden. In other words, you feel for the balance of the horse and transpose the pressure.

This should come down to general awareness; recognising the different effects of weight or pressure aids and understanding why, in every moment, every step of our riding, things may change. It is for this reason that I am so keen to instil in my students the logic behind the aids. Once we actually acknowledge what does what to the balance and body of the horse, we will develop much greater sensitivity and begin to know – with just the smallest

In applying the 'weight against' aid on the horse's side for lateral work or turning, the rider should never draw the knee and thigh outward, as shown here, since this will destabilise the seat.

Instead, draw the lower leg back so that the toe and knee remain forward facing, and simply press against the horse's side. Not only is this action more effective, it is also safer.

adjustment – how we can radically correct things even before they go wrong. It's another reason why expert riders can appear to work magic and transform an apparently difficult horse before its owner's eyes!

Too often the horse takes all the blame for being stiff on one side and hollow on the other, when in fact – if only they knew it – the rider has it within their power to correct this. It is simply a matter of thinking logically and feeling what type of pressure or weight aid the horse needs from us, at that particular moment in time. The choice is ours, and the responsibility, too!

All this should bring us to an understanding of lateral movements. Without that sense of feel, the aids will be pretty meaningless – not just to us, but to the horse, too. After all, we can read all the books in the world and be told the aids ad infinitum, but without understanding the logic of it all, we will never develop feel.

Up until now we have concentrated on improving our forward work. Apart from downward transitions, I have therefore tried to discourage readers from inadvertently stopping their horses with legs that cling on and hamper impulsion. When we move on to lateral work, this concept of freeing up the leg becomes even more important. Legs that are used to clamp on will be unable to give distinct pressure aids which now will be required not only to teach the horse to move away from the leg but, to a lesser degree, to support him on the other side. The most obvious example of using sideways pressure will be in the leg-yield or shoulder-in.

'Weight against' for sideways

There is nothing new about this concept of placing weight-against the horse since we use it all the time in the stable. If, for example, we apply pressure (weight) with our hand against his side, he will generally step sideways. This is a completely logical response and one which the young foal learns from his mother, almost as soon as he is born.

In riding, it is important to understand how sideways pressure can be used to our advantage – for example, when we wish to move the horse away from our weight as in the turn on the forehand, leg yield and shoulder-in.

Turn on the forehand

This gives the beginner the first taste of just how effective the sideways pressure of the inside leg can be in order to move the horse

Aids for turn on the forehand and leg yield are similar. The horse moves away from the pressure of the rider's inside leg (just behind the girth), and begins to step through with the inside hind, but bend is maintained through downward pressure, too.

away. This rudimentary exercise, ridden well away from the track, merely requires a displacement of our weight applied against the horse's flank, instead of allowing gravity to take it down uninterrupted.

With the horse stationary and supported to the outside, it is comparatively easy to ask the hindlegs to step over. To do the exercise correctly, however, the forelegs must mark time on the spot, so the sideways pressure from the leg must be applied carefully with clear pressure and release aids, step by step. The outside leg must be ready to support. Under no circumstances do we want the horse to swivel, so it's important the rider sits balanced but still, with a slight feeling of weight down in the inside sitrrup. Turn on the forehand is a very useful exercise for opening gates, but that is about as much as I recommend it – at least in the early stages of schooling.

Preparing for shoulder-in by riding a circle, Elaine demonstrates how too much weight-against will block engagement and unbalance both herself and the horse when he moves forwards and then sideways.

Leg yield

Instead of asking the horse to come more around the inside leg, the rider asks the horse to move away from the pressure, so that he is sent outward, over or sideways in the opposite direction. This is achieved by a gentle nudge against the horse's side, but the rider must be careful to remain centred and not to tilt to one side or the other, otherwise the message may be unclear or the horse becomes unbalanced.

Shoulder-in

This work should always be started in walk, although conventional dressage tests do not require shoulder-in until at least Elementary level, when it is ridden in trot. Many of the great masters introduced it as soon as the horse was forward going, accepting the bit – but not necessarily 'on the bit' – and confident in all three gaits. The idea being that an early introduction to the shoulder-in would help the horse come to the bit of his own volition, since the exercise strengthened him behind.

The shoulder-in requires us to achieve two different things at once, and this is where people often confuse their horses by remaining unaware of both requirements.

● Firstly, we ask the horse to bend into and around the rider's inside leg (downward pressure);

● secondly, we ask him to move away from the pressure of the same leg (weight-against).

At a glance, it seems this movement is a contradiction in terms, which is why I start riders on the ground, in order to develop 'feel'.

Provided the rider does not tilt, the sideways press with the inside leg should have an immediate effect on the equilibrium of the horse. As per the FEI directive, "the inside foreleg passes and crosses in front of the outside, and the inside hindleg steps in front of the outside hindleg". It is better not to ask for too much angle initially and to be clear, but succinct. Too strong a sideways push with the inside leg will unbalance both horse and rider.

As the horse becomes more experienced in shoulder-in, all the aids will be refined. On an experienced horse, the very act of turning the body into the required angle can often be enough. The weight-against feeling will become less and less until a well schooled horse can be moved away from the knee and thigh alone and the lower leg can assume it's normal position.

With the young horse, however, we must always be clear – that is why the weight-against, press and release aid is so important.

Always remember that a good shoulder-in may take many years to perfect and it is so much better if riders can start this work on a schoolmaster horse to discover the feel for themselves. When you first try it, be happy with just one or two steps at a time initially, and build up slowly.

On a young horse, riding both the circle and the shoulder-in in rising trot will help improve your own balance, and give the horse a chance to use his back and offer more behind.

For a great shoulder-in

Above, Lizzie demonstrates the main purpose of the shoulder-in: the stepping through and engagement of the horse's inside hind leg, and the lightening and freeing up of the horse's shoulders.

Prior to asking for the first sideways step, the rider must prepare the horse for what seems, at first, like a second circle. The idea is to free the horse's shoulders by riding the forehand one step off the track. Since the angle for shoulder-in is 30-35 degrees, the rider must align the upper body in the same way. There should be a nice feeling of bend in the girth from the inviting inside leg to encourage the necessary stepping through of the inside hindleg. Only then will the horse be able to move forward laterally in balance.

At the point where the circle could either continue or change into the lateral movement we must now make small adjustments;

● sit up very tall as though to check forward progression on the circle;
● echo this feeling in the outside rein, with a squeeze or half-halt. Then (with the young horse) think of opening this rein slightly to lead the horse along the track;
● maintain flexion with the inside rein, but keep the feeling very soft – no pulling back;
● bring the inside leg to bear (weight against) the horse's side just behind the girth in the form of a definite press or tap;
● support the angle with the outside knee and thigh – not pushing back at the horse – but passively, as though to 'catch' him in each sideways step;
● allow the outside lower leg to rest behind the girth to check the quarters;
● think 'step across' one step at a time and release the pressure of the inside leg between each request;
● think 'forward and sideways' with each step you take.

This three-track shoulder-in (below) shows the inside leg applied lightly just behind the girth. With the inside rein soft, the angle of the movement is obviously determined by the rider's seat and upper body position, not the hand.

What can go wrong?

Too much neck bend?

This will happen when the rider uses too much inside rein and has attempted to pull the forehand off the track rather than riding forward from behind into the first step of a new circle. Instead, ask for flexion from the fingers and in the first step of shoulder-in think of taking both hands gently into the direction of the movement. This will bring the inside rein against the wither (but don't allow it to cross) which will encourage the forehand to move in the opposite direction – almost a weight aid in itself.

Horse rushing sideways or lurching onto the outside shoulder?

This may happen if the rider fails to turn the outside hip, thigh and knee into the required angle. A gaping knee invites the horse to fall out. It is very important to support to the outside, but be careful not to block. Also, too much pressure from the inside leg will throw the horse off balance. The weight aids must always be subtle and applied on-off.

Horse unable to step 'through' with the inside hindleg?

Lack of engagement behind can be caused by lack of bend through the horse's ribcage, or because the rider is sitting too heavily to the inside. That is why we need to sit tall and centred in these movements – there is no point in thinking about shoulder-in until the horse is soft and supple on his circle work.

Horse trying to 'escape' and move off the track

Depending on the horse, it may help to sit very slightly more into the outside seatbone, after your first step of circle. If the horse feels your body taking him off the track he will follow – you must think more sideways and up the track to help him feel the same.

Here, Andorinha (aged 24) offers nice lateral steps in shoulder-in, but some of the energy is escaping onto the outside shoulder. When this happens, return to the circle to improve bend and engagement, and start again.

And finally...

Some trainers insist the rider faces up the track, but since your head weighs about 10 - 12 pounds, this can give an incorrect weight aid, pulling the horse back onto the track to straighten him out of his shoulder-in. In riding, you should always turn your head to face the same way as your horse, but there is no reason why your eyes should not glance up the track! Many pupils remark how changing their head position makes all the difference to the quality and ease of this lovely movement.

Shoulder-in – from the ground...

The rider must think of aligning the entire body at an angle of roughly 35 degrees to the wall or track. Take the weight on to the inside leg to lead forward, and then move it across, so that a sideways step is achieved. By practising this a few times, students soon get the feel of how their inside hip sightly deepens to engage, just as it does in the horse, and how important it is not to twist the upper body, but to keep everything – head, shoulders, waist, hips and knees – facing in the same direction.

... then back on board

The rider must also think of riding the movement in two stages, at least in the early days. Once the horse understands these two stages, you can virtually forget about them and the whole exercise will be ridden as one. However, in our initial schooling, it is important to show the horse the way with two distinct and different actions, both of which require a discreet change of weight to show the horse exactly what we want. These take the form of –

● downward pressure at the girth to invite the horse's forehand to move forward off the track and to bend around the inside leg;
● sideways pressure against the horse's side just behind the girth, to move the horse laterally.

Unfortunately, too many riders entirely forget the first aid, so intent are they upon applying the second. However, without first initiating bend, we will be in danger of merely pushing the horse's quarters out from under him, leading to a neck-in, rather than a shoulder-in.

A good rider will generally set the horse up for shoulder-in by preparing him on the circle – 12 to 10 metres being the norm. This is done with the normal circle aids, inside leg and inside seatbone slightly deepened, outside leg back to support the quarters. The smaller circle encourages greater suppling and engagement to set the horse up for the lateral movement.

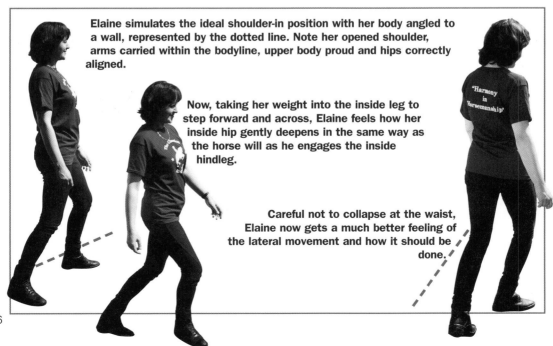

Elaine simulates the ideal shoulder-in position with her body angled to a wall, represented by the dotted line. Note her opened shoulder, arms carried within the bodyline, upper body proud and hips correctly aligned.

Now, taking her weight into the inside leg to step forward and across, Elaine feels how her inside hip gently deepens in the same way as the horse will as he engages the inside hindleg.

Careful not to collapse at the waist, Elaine now gets a much better feeling of the lateral movement and how it should be done.

Further thoughts on shoulder-in

As you turn your shoulders, be careful not to twist. Hold the sideways feel throughout your entire frame, remembering that the outside of your body affects the outside of your horse.

Sitting more on one seatbone or the other should never involve a collapse to the inside. To help with this, think of turning your sternum and navel, as well as the shoulders. With the shoulder blades open, bent elbows, and arms lightly contained within the bodyline, the reins should automatically assume the correct position.

The inside rein must not shorten and the rider should only feel sufficiently on the inside snaffle for a soft bend from the poll, never from the wither. The outside rein should support the horse and in the early stages there should be a slight sensation of it leading the horse along the track. Once the horse is more confirmed in his work, the outside rein is gently used to support the angle of the shoulders.

Once the horse is beginning to offer some pleasing lateral steps, advance to work in trot. There are two schools of thought about whether or not you should favour a particular seatbone once the work is confirmed. Of course, we should all be aiming to sit as centrally as possible all of the time, but things can change and much depends upon what your horse prefers. Riding other people's horses, I find I sit a little more into my inside seatbone if they have a tendency to lose bend and draw back to the track. But if they remain nicely bent but lack lateral impulsion, I sit more into the outside seatbone. On a well-schooled horse, I sit dead central!

Here, Espada shows a well defined three-track shoulder-in in trot. Ears back do not mean a black mood – he's just one of those horses always listening for the next request.

Chapter Eight

More lateral movements

In Chapter Seven we discussed the feel of applying pressure against the horse in order to ask him to step away from our inside leg. This displacement of weight is particularly useful in the turn on the forehand, leg yield and shoulder-in. Now we can think more widely about the role of the rider's outside leg. Most riders appreciate how important this aid is in the canter strike-off (see Chapter Six) and how it helps to encourage stretch to the outside in circles and corners. The outside leg is, of course, always invaluable for keeping the horse's quarters under control in a very general sense.

We have also discussed the role of the outside leg used more specifically to turn the horse away from the track. Whether this is done in walk, trot or canter, the whole process of turning will become so much more effective and immediate once we think in terms of working outside in, as well as inside out.

Quarter-pirouette

To improve both our own and the horse's understanding of the weight-against principle of the outside leg, now is the time to introduce the quarter-pirouette. This is used to move off the school wall or centre line to form a right angle. A good suppling and manoeuvring exercise, it prepares the horse for further lateral work.

The quarter-pirouette comprises a turn on the haunches or turn on the hocks of 90 degrees (the half-pirouette being 180 degrees). Whilst the hindlegs should take two small forward and sideways steps virtually on the spot, the forelegs take two much more sweeping and definite steps around them. In other words, the weight of the horse is transposed to the hind end, whilst the forehand is freed up to move around it. Ridden from the track at E, for example, completion of the turn will mean the horse faces straight across to B.

Preparing for a right quarter-pirouette (or turn on the hocks), Elaine glances right, sits a little deeper into the right seatbone, then turns her horse away from the track with the (unseen) outside leg to face the opposite direction.

The effective weight-against aid of the outside (left) leg starts at the rider's outside hip. The left knee and thigh also play a supportive role in the turn on the hocks to the right. Note also the influence of the outside rein.

The aids for the turn are virtually the opposite to the aids for the turn on the forehand (described in the last chapter). Indeed, once the horse has learned to turn away from the track easily and with minimum fuss, the turn on the hocks should become semi-automatic. Think how many horses naturally spin on their hocks when they want to get out of harm's way! By capitalising on our horse's natural instincts it is much easier to teach him something new. However, the real beauty of this movement is that it teaches the horse to bring his hindlegs more under him so that he can balance with his weight back, but without stress! This, coupled with the shoulder-in, is one of the best ways of developing collection in the early days. Not only does it encourage greater bending through the hindlimb joints, but it frees up the horse's shoulders, leading to lightness in hand.

Whilst horses have little difficulty with this way of turning, it is harder sometimes to teach the rider. Riders who have always believed that control starts in the horse's mouth will be the hardest to convince. For that reason, it is important to approach the aids step by step...

On the ground

Here I demonstrate how we must lead from the inside for the walk or canter pirouette (right). For the horse to turn in balance, the rider's inside hip must stay forward whilst the outside (left) hip drives the horse round the turn. All this is helped by projecting upward and forward from the abdominals, with the shoulders back.

for most exercises is that, generally, as one leg activates, the other 'allows', supports or receives. In all riding, there should always be an obvious opening through which the horse may pass, and in this case it will be to the inside.

Making progress

Once your horse is turning away from the weight-against influence of your outside leg, and bending nicely round your inside leg, ride some serpentines in trot. Using similar aids to those described, you'll be surprised how much more accurate you become. This will make your turns onto the centre line more effective, too.

When I'm preparing to ride down the centre line at A, I wait until my outside hand is almost level with the letter; then I use the weight-down aid to the inside, coupled with the weight-against aid of my outside leg and the horse turns, almost on the spot. Students find this exercise enlightening when they realise that a balanced turn has little to do with the inside rein, and much more to do with the outside leg and outside rein.

Once the quarter-pirouette is accomplished easily, the rider may progress at a much later stage to half-pirouette comprising four separate steps. However, this is an advanced movement and should not be tackled until ready. Whilst it can be ridden on the track, we have to be very careful not to allow the horse to step back and bruise his hocks on the arena wall. For this reason, it is generally ridden across the manège since a correct half-pirouette is much easier said than done. At an even higher level of training, canter pirouette can be introduced, and the principles involved for walk pirouettes will remain the same.

For a great quarter-pirouette

● The rider ensures that the inside leg is at the girth; this leg plays a supportive but fairly passive role.
● The rider sits tall and square; there should be a little more weight into the inside seatbone and pressure in the inside stirrup.
● The horse is gently asked to flex from the poll – in other words, just to look to the inside.
● The rider moves the outside leg back – about a hand's distance behind the girth – and the whole leg applies a firm pressing aid against the horse's side.
● At the same time, the rider checks gently on the outside rein.
● The outside rein then guides the forehand into the direction of movement by closing towards the base of the neck.
● The whole feel should be that you work the horse from the outside inwards – then straighten!

Remember...

As with all our movements to date, we have to be aware of exactly how and where our weight is acting on the horse's body. The rule of thumb

What can go wrong?
● All this sounds very easy, but over-riding will lead to blocking.
● Twisting or collapsing the upper body may push the horse in the opposite direction.
● A tight inside leg will prevent the horse moving into and around it.
● Too much inside rein will cause the horse to jackknife outward through the shoulders.
● A backward application of the outside rein will prevent him leaving the track.
● Giving away the outside rein may cause the horse to fall onto the forehand.
● Squeezing or tensing the outside leg may cause the knee to gape open, leaving an opening for the horse to stray out to the track, instead of turning. Make sure the whole leg, knee and thigh too, quietly closes in.

Travers
Once the horse is moving nicely away from the weight-against aid, try introducing travers (or quarters-in). This is not generally taught until the horse is absolutely supple and adept at shoulder-in, as it could lead to him working with his quarters in during his straight work. Travers should never be ridden more than shoulder-in and top dressage riders use it sparingly, mainly as a preparation for half-pass.

Travers is best ridden from a 10-metre circle to stimulate bend and forwardness. As you move back to the track, the horse's head and shoulders continue to face the direction of travel by flexing into the inside rein; the quarters are prevented from rejoining the track by the rider's outside leg. This promotes a deeper engagement of the horse's inside hindlimb joints which bears the weight as he steps over and through with the outside hind. Travers can be ridden on three or four tracks, as shown.

Here I am riding six-year-old Prazer in the correct left travers, showing good tracking and bend.

Practice makes perfect
Travers is often easier for horses and riders on one rein than the other. It is best practised in the early days slightly away from the track, as it can be very daunting for the horse to be ridden right up to a wall or fence, then be expected to move laterally! Practise it yourself on the ground to achieve the angle! Feel how you sink your weight more into the leading leg, but how you press over more with the outside one.

For a great travers
● **The rider's body gives the horse the angle (roughly 35 degrees) to the track along which he should proceed laterally.**
● **Leading with the inside hip, the rider steps a little deeper into the inside leg, which remains at the girth.**
● **The rider gently feels on the inside rein to** lead the forehand down the track.
● **The rider gently checks with the outside rein to prevent the horse turning fully onto the track, then guides the forehand into the direction of travel.**
● **The outside leg presses the horse sideways behind the girth.**
● **The rider thinks forward and sideways and rides accordingly.**

Early attempts at travers often result in tilting or tipping forward, which will block the horse and make him reluctant to move forward to the fence.

Here, horse and rider start the exercise away from the fence to establish confidence; at this stage it is better not to try for too much bend.

If travers fails in the first attempts, it is often because the rider is not sitting up or keeping the inside hip bone forward. Too many riders tilt and block, so do things gradually – and always lighten up and ride forward into your circle when things go wrong.

Half-pass

The half-pass is another movement involving an effective use of the weight-down and weight-against syndrome. As with circles, turns and travers, the rider's inside leg leads by deepening slightly, and again it is the outside leg which moves back and against the horse to encourage him sideways.

In half-pass, an advanced lateral movement, the horse needs to lead with the forehand, but to cross both front and hindlegs with each step. He is also expected to look and bend into the direction of travel, and all this requires succinct, downward weight aids to the inside.

Prepare your horse by starting from a 10-metre circle, this time ridden from the centre line, and proceed in a diagonal direction back to

Once this is understood, more bend can be requested with the rider sitting tall, supporting the bend through a slightly weighted inside stirrup, and positively showing the way forward and sideways.

83

Eyes look into
the movement

Supporting inside
leg and weight
into inside
stirrup

Horse soft and
attentive

Horse and
rider square to
centre line

Here, we see half-pass
practised in walk,
showing a more
collected horse which
remains virtually parallel
to the centre line
(corrrect), while
maintaining good bend
around my inside leg.

Outside rein
moving horse
gently left

Outside leg
activating
outside hind

Good
crossing

What can go wrong?

- A collapsed upper body may push the rider's weight to the outside, so the half-pass or travers never gets started in the first place.
- Looking over the horse's outside shoulder (a very common fault) will make him want to bend the wrong way.
- If the rider's inside hip drifts back, instead of 'leading', the horse may go into a form of leg yield.
- Too much outside leg may push the horse onto his inside shoulder or allow him to lead with the quarters.
- Too much inside leg (weight-against the horse) will block the sideways progression.
- Insufficient weight-down and asking from the inside leg will negate bend and direction.

- An unyielding outside rein may compound these problems by turning the horse's head away from the movement.

The knock-on effects of incorrect aiding, weight distribution and a lack of feel are endless. Half-pass and travers are not easy movements to ride, and you can't be expected to get it right at once. For this reason, when teaching travers and half-pass for the first time, I tell my pupils to keep the horse's head almost straight to start, and to concentrate on the direction and forward-sideways feeling. Once they can send the horse roughly where they want from the legs and body, it's then quite an easy matter to sort out the hands and improve the head position with the correct feeling of flexion to the inside.

the track. The track represents a visual guide to help you keep your horse's body relatively parallel to it, and offers the horse a sense of security as he moves towards it.

Aids for half-pass

- Sit tall and roughly square, but think 'lead' with your inside hip, and incline your head in the direction of travel.
- Feel and gently open the inside rein, but not enough to displace and twist the neck.
- Step a little down into the inside stirrup (toe aligned at the girth) with pressure on the ball of the foot. Again, indicate 'lead with your weight' and do not block the horse to the inside.
- The outside rein gently checks the progress of the forehand to the inside; it may also nudge against the wither to help move the horse's shoulders across.
- The whole outside leg moves back and presses (weight-against) the horse's side to encourage him to step away in the opposite direction.
- Once the horse is moving laterally, use small, light touches with the inside leg for bend and impulsion, but remember you must still support and 'lead' the forehand forward.

It is the combination of all the aids working together which keeps the horse together in half-pass. Timing is vital, and more than ever before we should be thinking of the different 'ask and receive' roles of our body.

Getting started with half-pass

When starting half-pass, teach the movement in walk and only attempt one or two steps at a time. Then straighten and go forward. (Only attempt trot when the horse really understands the aids, as it takes time to establish the rhythm and balance required.) Later, start from the corner of the manège, ride a 10-metre circle, half-pass to the quarter line, straighten, circle again, half-pass to the centre line and repeat until you arrive at the far corner on the other side.

When you come to ride several steps of half-pass together across a long diagonal, help yourself through visualisation. It is all too easy to move too much sideways, without progressing forward, so imagine a wall running diagonally back to the track and ride forward and sideways along it. This really helps. It is the successful synchronisation of all these aids which will lead to success in half-pass. But it is only by knowing and recognising exactly what the horse feels when you apply these aids, that things will become clear.

In the half-pass, it is the deepening and allowing of the inside leg which encourages the horse to move towards it. By the same token, it is the asking of the outside leg and the pressure it applies against the horse's side which sends him into the movement. Think of 'feeding' your horse into the inside leg from your outside leg when you ride half-pass and travers,

Lateral work not only improves all the gaits, it paves the way for lengthening and extension. Here, I ride medium trot out of the shoulder-in – what a pity I am looking down!

From a gentle half-halt, upper body tall – this collected trot can launch a really forward uphill extension.

and once you start thinking like this, you will be amazed at the difference it makes.

Collection towards extension

Never forget that, right from the beginning, riding the lateral movements will require a degree of collection. Whether riding shoulder-in, turn on the hocks, travers or half-pass, try gently to half-halt with your upper body in each forward and sideways step, with only a very mild feel on the rein. Doing things this way gives the horse time and space to step through, even to dwell momentarily on the weight-bearing inside hind leg. Remember, however, that it is the movements themselves which develop and enhance the collection process - which is our main purpose for using them!

Once the horse can really move through and engage in these exercises, his whole frame will start to round and lift. This is where your posture becomes even more important so you can encourage collection to blossom and grow. This lightening effect gives greater scope to the reach of the hindlegs so all the gaits should now improve. Good lengthening can only come from strong hindquarters and well-engaged hindlegs, and the lateral movements are a wonderful launchpad for developing the medium and extended gaits. It's simply a matter of gently checking, then unleashing the energy we have built and conserved so carefully.

Do not be deceived by people who tell you to nag, or drive the horse into a longer frame. A harsh, pushing seat will tend in time to weaken the horse's back and, in the case of a sensitive horse, drive him into the forehand. Instead, prepare for lengthened strides by setting your horse more on the hocks with a gentle half-halt; then, as you feel the back raise and the shoulders lighten, you know this is the moment to allow the impulsion through.

In this way we learn that collection and extension has little to do with restricting the front end, it's all to do with mobilising and strengthening the hind end – all of which will benefit from a skilful use of your weight aids. You should now be well on your way to achieving a balanced, supple, forward-going and happy horse.

Chapter Nine

Counter-canter

Now that we have understood the concept of moving the horse away from the outside leg, as in the pirouette or turn on the hocks, travers and half-pass, we will be in a much better postion to refine the canter.

I have already stressed that moving the horse away from pressure requires that we counter-balance by supporting to the opposite side. However, as previously stated, the horse must never feel trapped between the aids, and this is where real feel must be developed. As we support we must also learn to assess how much to allow at the same time; indeed, there will be many occasions when the horse needs to be encouraged to move more into our space. So

whether that allowing feeling is applied through the rein, seat or leg (generally all three working together) the principle is much the same; it is the take and give of each aid which shows the horse where to go, and nowhere is this more important and relevant to the horse than in the canter, and especially the counter-canter.

As a schooling technique, the counter-canter is a brilliant suppling exercise and is particularly good for strengthening and increasing muscle tone in the horse's loins. Indeed, it is an excellent way of building up the topline of the horse generally. Most dressage tests, from Elementary level upwards, will demand at least some strides of counter-canter, and apart from that it is another step forward in the growing understanding between you and the horse.

Canter falling apart?

Whilst few people have difficulty in normal canter with the correct canter strike-off on a corner or circle, and can keep their horses nicely balanced as long as they are riding on a curve, problems often occur on a straight line.

This is generally because they have forgotten to maintain a degree of bend. Too often riders remove the very support that the horse requires from the inside leg when they ask their horse to canter 'large' and return to the long side of the arena. This is a serious mistake because the horse will be unprepared when he comes into the next corner, and he may well panic and change leads behind in an attempt to deal with

Many people think that by relaxing down into the horse, they will make it easier for him. The contrary is true! Collapsing the abdominals and dropping the diaphragm will lead to uneven weight pressure, which may block the horse and make it very difficult to bend round the leading leg. Instead, centralise and think up, weight down!

Support

Due to the nature of canter, when sometimes there is only one leg on the ground and, during the moment of suspension, none at all, it is vital the rider assists the horse to stay in balance. Good bend must be established prior to moving on to counter-canter. The more difficult the movement, the more the horse will rely on the support of the rider's inside leg to provide a 'connection' to the ground. However, subtlety continues to be the name of the game and we must be very careful not to tip the balance of the 'pair of scales' too far, one way or the other.

For this reason, it is time to become more aware of the significance of the inside leg position and how it works. The action of deepening or 'stepping down' with the inside leg at the girth should bring about the following complementary effects. It should:

● lengthen the muscles of the inside thigh, which deepens the knee and allows greater support from the inside thighbone which remains close and supportive. This will help prevent the horse 'falling in' through the inside shoulder.

● free the rider's lower leg just away from the horse's side to make room for the horse to jump through into canter with the correct leading foreleg.

● increase the weight-down feeling into the inside seatbone (and/or stirrup) which again indicates lead and direction.

As usual the maxim is simple – if you want your horse to move left, he must feel that your aids take him left.

Even in normal canter around the arena, never forget to continue supporting the horse with the inside leg deepened at the girth.

the balancing act he is then expected to make. Even if he doesn't change, inconsistent aiding may well result in a horse becoming heavier and heavier in the hand as the canter progresses. He cannot realistically be blamed for this, for if you take away one support, he will require another – the hands!

Leaning on the forehand is generally caused either by the rider collapsing forward or, more commonly, forgetting to support the horse with the inside leg after the first upward transition. It can, however, be caused by weakness in the horse's back, and with young horses in particular they may not have sufficient topline muscle tone to sustain more than half a circuit or so of canter in good balance. For this reason, it is important to practise lots of transitions – trot to canter, walk to canter and canter to trot – to lighten the forehand and discourage flattening out and rushing.

Canter to walk is more advanced than walk to canter and not normally requested until the horse has been introduced to counter-canter, which greatly assists his balance. This is a time for refining your weight aids, and ensuring that your outside leg applies sufficient pressure to keep the horse's hocks active and under him so that he really can learn to engage. You must also continue to support the horse to the inside through every phase of his canter, but be careful that your inside leg does not take over the role of the outside.

The inside leg should be relatively passive in canter turns and bends. It should maintain its position at the girth (think of a pillar) around which the horse can balance and yield his body. Since pillars carry their weight downward, and generally don't move, it can be counterproductive at this stage to squeeze with the inside leg for more impulsion. Undoubtedly, very discreet touches at the girth will stimulate, but if you cannot trust yourself to do this in the correct place, it may be better to use a little more seat and/or outside leg. What must be clear to the horse is the support to the inside and a sense of being led. Since our leg position is reflected in our hip position, any deviation may cause a loss of balance. Too many riders employ a flapping inside leg and wonder why the horse falls back to trot. Others are nudged sideways, which may cause a 'green' or sensitive horse to change legs behind, so play it safe and let your leg be a pillar!

Preparing for counter-canter

If you have really worked on your aids in Chapter Six, introducing counter-canter should be relatively easy for the horse to understand. We can start by cantering loops of three metres in from the track and back out again (shown by the blue line on the diagram). As the horse becomes more laterally supple, these loops may be increased to five metres (shown in pink on the diagram), so the horse is encouraged to work away from the track and back onto it, without changing legs.

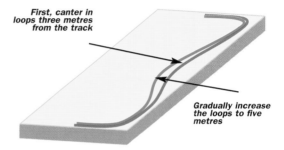

First, canter in loops three metres from the track

Gradually increase the loops to five metres

Mental adjustments

Long ago, as a teenager, I remember watching a dressage test at Badminton Horse Trials and marvelling at a horse circling in counter-canter. To me then, this seemed the most difficult thing in the world! Yet if we think about canter from the horse's point of view, we will begin to realise that there is no 'right' or 'wrong' leg for him, so perhaps it isn't such a miracle after all.

Once we go back to nature, it becomes obvious that cantering on the 'correct leg' is a man-made concept, and most horses can canter relatively easily on both leads. It's quite common to see a horse in the field cantering on the opposite lead to the direction in which he is going, without bothering to change, so why is it so difficult for us?

Go left – think 'right'!

The problem for most students new to this exercise is that they are convinced they must 'think' left the moment they go on to the left rein. However, counter-canter on the left rein involves right lead, so the first thing we need to do is to think of the lead – irrespective of the rein. If we don't make this mental adjustment, it will be very difficult for the horse to give us what we want.

Too often, our bodies are still focused on the direction in which we're going, so the horse feels us 'cantering' the other way round. But what do I mean by our bodies cantering? Surely we don't have to pretend to canter on horseback? Actually, in a sense, we do! I don't mean that we should be jumping about – quite the contrary – we must continue to sit upright, supportive and as still as possible.

Nevertheless, if we don't adopt a position which mirrors the way we set ourselves up to canter (or skip) on the ground, we will make it difficult for our horses to give us what we want. Ideally, the horse should feel that our hips and legs are in a position where we could skip or canter with him. If we are against him – and our bodies are 'cantering' on the wrong lead – we will be very much at odds with each other.

It is at this point that we will need, mentally and physically, to reconfirm our canter aids. Canter is such a finely balanced gait – at one phase the horse is suspended in the air, and in another he is balancing on one leg – so control of our weight becomes even more important than ever. Indeed, a slippage of weight, a few

ounces this way or that, can make the whole exercise of counter-canter impossible for the horse. It is for this reason that so many people encounter problems.

Reconfirming the canter aids (on the ground)

Let us re-examine, in very simple terms, what the horse has to do in normal canter on the right lead. He will push off with his left hind and appear to 'lead' with his right fore. It is these two aspects of canter that really matter as far as feeling is concerned, so set aside the exact sequence of footfalls.

In Chapter Six we discussed confirming the correct weight aids for normal canter by practising on the ground first. We discovered how, in pushing off with our outside (left) leg drawn back, we needed to step or jump forward into the right leg to lead that way. In riding terms, this involved keeping our inside (right) hip forward, and gently letting our weight down into the inside (right) stirrup, which stayed aligned under the hip, close to the girth.

When we consider counter-canter, we still

Here, I have just straightened Espada out of the corner in counter-canter. All the time I am thinking canter right, even though we are on the left rein. My (unseen) right leg is at the girth, my left leg a little behind the girth. If you look closely, I am just looking right, my right hip is forward and the left hip slightly back, as in normal canter right.

In the next frame, you can see I have lightened the weight on the back of the saddle to encourage the engaging hind leg. We should do this in normal canter too, only this would obviously be to the outside and unseen from the centre of the school.

need to ask the horse to canter right or left, irrespective of whichever rein he is on, so the aids must remain the same.

If all this sounds too easy, the truth is – it is. Changes only occur if the horse has not learned to trust your aids in normal canter, in which case carrying them through into counter-canter will be meaningless. (In such a case you will need to spend more time in normal canter.) If, however, the horse is secure in canter right or canter left, he should stay in the same canter and the same bend. Provided we hold our own canter position therefore, he should hold his. By allowing and supporting with our aids rather than over-demanding, we give him room to manoeuvre, so changing the rein should not make too much difference. Nevertheless, first attempts do require extra rider confidence. You must always check that you are doing everything correctly and believe that the horse will follow you.

To reconfirm normal canter right: place your hands on your hips, skip, and feel how the inside hip moves forward to complement the supporting inside leg. Then, simply maintain this feeling in counter-canter (left rein).

Changing legs, falling back to trot or going disunited generally only occur when the rider changes the balance, removes support to the inside, or simply stops riding forwards. If the horse changes legs it's likely that one of our checkpoints has failed. Don't panic; simply try again with minimum fuss.

Initially, keep the angle of the return to the track relatively shallow. Too acute an angle may scare the horse and force a change. Think of sliding the horse back onto the track, rather than confronting it head on. That is why it's important that your eyes look forward and through his ears, so you gaze over and beyond the leading leg, rather than at the arena fence.

What else can go wrong?

If the horse tries to change in front or behind, it is generally because:
● **your weight has shifted to the outside seatbone (generally caused by leaning inwards or over-turning in the half circle).**
● **too much inside hand has blocked the horse's leading inside shoulder.**
● **your inside leg has shot forward, with the same result.**
● **insufficient easing of the outside rein has prevented the necessary stretching in the turn and half-circle.**
● **too much movement in the seat has nullified the aids.**
● **too much weight aid has upset the balance.**

If the horse runs into trot, it is generally because:
● **the rider's seat has slipped back, blocking the inside supporting hindleg.**
● **the inside leg is no longer supporting at the girth, so the horse has tipped onto the forehand.**
● **the rider's head and upper body have squared too suddenly onto the track, instead of looking over the leading leg.**

For a great counter-canter

Imagine we start on the 'correct' rein for canter right. The idea is to canter normally down the track (shown in blue on the diagram); then to make a 10 or 12 metre half-circle at H to the centre line; returning to and along the track at E with a few strides in counter-canter (now going left), before finishing in trot before the next corner.

● Before going large, first canter a 20 or 15 metre right circle at the end of the school to establish rhythm, forwardness and bend.

● As you move out to the track, remind yourself of the aids – a little more weight into the inside (right) seatbone; inside leg supporting at the girth; outside leg encouraging stretch; soft flexion through the inside rein, the rider looking slightly right.

● Proceed down the track to H, maintaining all these feelings and riding forward!

● Just before H, make a 10 or 12 metre half circle right to the centre line, aiding your horse with your outside leg and outside rein (as in turns off the track) while you sit tall, deepening the 'pillar' of your inside leg and resisting any temptation to lean in!

● Facing back to the track via the diagonal, keep your upper body supported, especially through the inside hip, and think of your deep right leg and weighted seatbone 'leading' your horse to E, whilst the outside leg and rein encourages his return.

● Maintain this weighted feeling as you ride parallel to the track but retain a slight feeling of right bend throughout. Your right rein should be light as you continue to look over the horse's inside (now the outside) leading leg.

● Ride boldly forward and believe your horse will remain in canter right – even though he is now travelling on the left rein. Remember, you too are cantering right; if nothing has changed in your own body, it should not change in the horse.

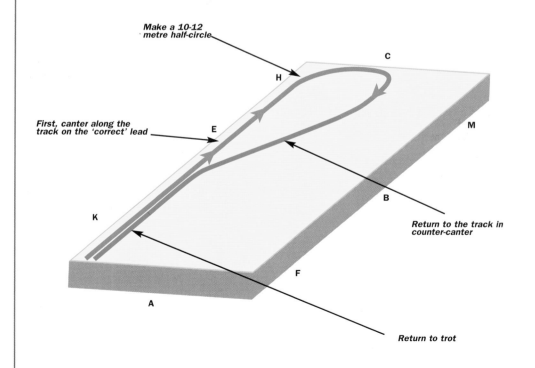

Make a 10-12 metre half-circle

First, canter along the track on the 'correct' lead

Return to the track in counter-canter

Return to trot

The benefits of counter-canter will be shown in true canter. Here, we see Espada ridden in medium canter through a corner, showing good balance and power thanks to the depth of engagement of the inside hindleg. We must always do our best to support but never to block when our horses offer us so much. (Warning – don't try this until the horse is really confident and strong through the back.)

Small things matter!

People are often amazed that something so seemingly small as changing where you look can make such a difference. Yet some of the world's best dressage horses will make tempi changes just on a nod to left or right from the rider. We must realise that apart from the actual weight of the head and neck, focusing one way or the other does bring about imperceptible small changes in the rest of our body. So stay looking over the leading leg until you wish to end the counter-canter. This will be one of the few times you should look to the outside of the track, so make the most of it!

Don't try too much!

Once you have successfully managed a couple of steps of counter-canter along the track, bring your horse back to trot before the corner. So often counter-canter is lost – as is the confidence of the horse – because people have asked for too much. Two or three steps is very encouraging and you should praise the horse. Try this exercise on both reins, but only continue round the corner when you really feel the work is well understood. This may take months, but it will be worth it in the end.

Powering on in medium

Counter-canter is excellent for strengthening the horse's back behind the saddle (the loins) and, once he is able to hold the counter-canter round a corner, you can really feel him stretch and round these muscles. A word of warning, however, never ride too many strides in counter-canter. Always return to normal canter in

At a more advanced level, counter-canter can be ridden on the circle. Here, Espada is in counter-canter but has slightly tilted his head since the circle makes it difficult to look over the leading leg.

between and work more on your transitions within the gait. In Chapter Six we talked about introducing some strides of medium canter along the long side of the arena and out hacking. Now is the time to gradually introduce circles in medium canter. A good way to start is to make the first half of a 20m circle in a more collected canter, then ride the second half in medium. This will not only improve suppleness and balance, but will make the exercise more interesting and fun for the horse.

By the time you are negotiating corners in medium canter, you will be much more aware of the benefits of counter-canter and how it has helped the general power and engagement of your horse in true canter.

Counter-canter on the circle

Provided the horse is balanced and able to remain in a steady rhythm, you should be ready to progress to counter-canter on the half-circle, full circle and, finally, right round the school. The more demanding the exercise, the more you may have to emphasise the feeling of weight to the inside (now the outside) 'leading' stirrup. Remember, in riding terms, inside generally relates to bend – not the inside of the arena!

Be aware that every horse is different. Horses that are naturally inclined to canter, such as Arabs, Thoroughbreds and some Warmbloods, often find counter-canter fairly easy. Others bred for their trotting ability, such as cobs and carriage breeds, find it more

A few strides on, Espada straightens his neck and I deepen the inside leg forward and ask for a flying change from the counter-canter. The camera captures the moment where he organises his hindlimbs to make the change behind.

Most horses are only too happy to offer the change out of a demanding exercise and return to a normal circle – as we see from Espada's pricked ears and onward bound expression!

challenging. Then there are the horses that have spent years not being allowed to canter on the 'wrong' leg. They are going to find it quite surprising to be asked to do things differently, especially if they have previously been reprimanded for doing so. Counter-canter on the circle is not only a great suppling exercise, it is also a great way of setting the horse up for flying changes. Although all horses do these naturally, it's very different from making a change at a specified spot in the show or dressage arena – and on request, as we shall see in the next chapter!

Last minute checks

Whenever and however you ride counter-canter, there are a number of checks you should make:

● Am I still looking over the horse's leading leg?

● Is my body 'thinking' into that same lead?

● Is my original inside leg still stepping down (even though it is now on the outside)?

● Is it supporting the original bend?

● Is my original outside leg still acting its role (even though it's now on the inside)?

● Is it encouraging the horse from behind so he doesn't break into trot, or become disunited?

● Has my original outside hip remained open to let the horse 'through'?

● Is the angle too acute, or the circle too tight?

Chapter Ten

Flying changes, passage, piaffe

If our training has been clear and consistent, we should by now feel that our horse has become totally sensitised to our weight. Just a little pressure here and a little less there creates an effect. Our horse will recognise the difference between moving away from pressure, and moving into pressure.

Riding from the centre

With this increased sensitivity, the rider should feel that the horse is, at all times, working through from behind. The idea that the aids can stimulate or re-channel impulsion is based on the fact that the rider pilots the horse from the centre. This means that changes in balance can be made at any time. So we learn to harness the energy produced by the horse's 'engine' and utilise it for our various purposes, long before it reaches the forehand.

When it comes to hacking out, hunting and cross-country, some believe that the rider should 'follow' the horse. This generally makes sense –

The subtle approach

For our aids to be easily felt and recognised by the horse so that the work literally looks invisible with minimum fuss, the rider must always sit quietly and centrally. As with a see-saw, we cannot control the equilibrium of the horse if there is no steady, central support to the structure. Let us recap on the various points which allow us to maximise on the methods described in this book.

● We must sit over the strongest point of the horse's back – just behind the wither – supporting our upper bodies (use your backbone!) in both the forward and full seat.
● This requires remaining as close to the pommel as possible – and we will need a saddle that allows us to do this!
● We must let the weight of our legs fall away from us by gravity, so that we are in balance with ourselves.
● We must be as natural in our balance (without ever having to force things) as when we stand, walk, jog, skip or run.
● In riding, our connection to the ground should transfer itself via the seat into the stirrups.

● This allows the 'springs' (our joints) to absorb movement so we can flow with the horse.
● If our feet are not directly under our hips when we ride, our weight may impact too much on the horse's back.
● Whether we block through the crotch or the back of the seat, the recycling effect of the horse's energy will be interrupted.
● Only from a more neutral, centred position can we apply discreet weight aids with immediate effect.

Remember, however, that changes of weight and pressure must only be applied as and when the occasion demands it, so the actual action is minute. Timing is of the essence, thinking what is required almost before it happens. In this way, the aids become mere echoes of the thought and feel process. We should always feel we are just ahead of the horse so we can anticipate what he requires from us; this gives him time to organise his body in response to each request. As we become mirror images of one another, we remember that in dressage it must be the horse that mirrors us.

once you've set your horse up and taken a line. However, changes of weight will always be required for a change of direction, pace or terrain.

Too often, riders blame the horse if things go wrong, yet errors are usually the result of incorrect aiding. For example, not even a well-schooled horse can make a balanced turn if the rider's bodyweight is misplaced, Stiffness in the horse is generally an inheritance of rider error, so if the 'conventional' aids are not complemented by the correct weight aids, the horse may continue to make mistakes. Luckily, most horses are forgiving and it's never too late to improve. In this chapter, we look at how to achieve the more advanced movements.

The flying change

When the time comes to teach flying changes – when the horse changes canter lead in the air between strides – the ability to make ourselves clear to the horse through our weight is vital. If the horse always associates canter right with feeling our bodyweight adjust right, then it should not be too difficult for him to associate a change of leg through a change in ourselves. Unfortunately, most people will tend to overdo this in the early days, forgetting the golden rule that the weight aids must be subtle if they are to create the correct effect.

Ideally, your upper body should remain quiet and still as you make the changes through your seat and legs. Remember again, however, that when we change our canter position, we will also be changing the way in which our hips are aligned. It is the influence of our weight felt under the saddle that makes the changes in our leg position so effective and clear to the horse.

Most people introduce changes by first riding canter across the diagonal, making a downward transition at X into trot or walk, and then an upward transition into canter on the opposite leg; the idea is then to miss out the transitional steps and ask for the flying change. Whilst this

Out of the counter-canter and in the moment of suspension, I move my 'new' inside leg (right) forward and step down at the girth as my 'new' outside leg (left) moves back. In this way, Espada can spring from counter-canter into the new right lead, which will start behind.

way may seem logical to us, it will not necessarily be logical to the horse, who may be more motivated towards the transition than staying in canter. My own thinking is that if we can ask at a moment where the horse would prefer to change – in order to reach a comfort zone – then this could be a good way forward to introduce a new movement.

Finding an easy way

One of the easiest ways to teach your first flying change to the horse is from counter-canter (see Sylvia and Espada in the last chapter). This was shown on a circle but it is best introduced after the corner(s), which is what we'll consider here.

Let's say you are in left lead and are progressing along the track, bending left but on the right rein. Having successfully negotiated the first corner of the short side and remained in counter-canter, decide to ride your first change into right canter a couple of strides after the second corner.

The long side of the arena stretches invitingly ahead and since counter-canter is quite tiring for the horse, he will naturally find it easier to change. Two corners ridden in counter-canter is really challenging, since holding the bend to the outside will have stretched his somewhat under-used loin muscles to the limit. A change of leg, therefore, is very much the easy option – so what could be more natural than to be invited to change onto the 'correct' lead.

Once you appreciate that all you are asking is to normalise the canter, everything becomes much more logical, especially to the horse.

Personal preference

Flying changes are a very personal thing and this is one area where there may be differences of opinion about the sequence of the aids. There are also many different ways of asking for a change and some people prefer to teach it on a figure-of-eight. This is an excellent way when the horse understands what is required of him, but the horse may end up swinging crookedly from change to change, since often the rider demands so much bend.

To make changes easy for the horse, keep him as straight as possible. It was Colonel Podhajsky, that legendary figure of the Spanish Riding School, who always said; *"First straighten your horse."* Of course, in jumping or riding cross-country, many horses will change naturally when the rider changes balance or direction. But

For a great flying change

So back to counter-canter on the right rein. Your horse is bent to the left and leading with the left fore.

● First, straighten your horse; it's important that the head and neck are now looking directly forward instead of being slightly flexed over the leading (outside) leg.

● Draw up slightly and apply a gentle half-halt to place your horse a little more on his hocks.

● Now allow forward with the inside (right) rein, and at the same time lighten your seat by easing the upper body very slightly forward.

● Think change! – just as you would yourself as in skipping, where you jump into the new balance – with the opposite (right) hip and leg taking over the lead.

By now, the complementary leg and seat aids should be instinctive, but to recap, it will mean:

● the right (inside) leg steps forward and deepens at the girth

● the left (outside) leg 'opens' and moves back

● the weight is now slightly into your right (inside) seatbone

● the left (outside) leg activates the outside hind to jump through from behind and into the new right lead.

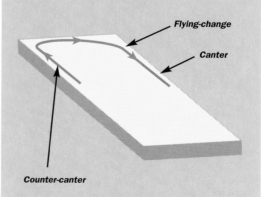

Flying-change

Canter

Counter-canter

making changes in a dressage arena on demand is something else completely. You should take your time and the horse should never be punished if he makes a mistake.

What can go wrong?

The most common problem when teaching your horse changes is that you effect a change of leg in front, but not behind. This can be caused by any of the following lapses:
● **rider sitting too heavy or leaning back, blocking the new incoming hindleg;**
● **rider's outside hip is too tight; there should be a sense of opening the joints to the outside to make room for the horse to jump through from behind;**
● **rider moving about too much and muffling the clarity of the aids.**

If the horse simply refuses to change at all, or ignores the aids, you may have to re-assess the canter work in general. There may be numerous causes:
● **horse on forehand – insufficient balance and engagement even to try;**
● **rider moving the legs appropriately, but nuances of change through hips not clear;**
● **over-riding (a very common mistake) and unbalancing the horse with huge shifts of weight through the upper body – swinging the shoulders is popular!**

Flying changes may look easy for a horse in freedom or with a good rider on the horse's back, but we have to recognise they are very gymnastic exercises and should not be undertaken until the horse is ready. The subject is complex and there are many finer points which can be developed with careful exercises and study, but help may be required from outside. My book, *Dressage in Lightness – Speaking the Horse's Language,* gives more in-depth advice, but provided we realise no horse can change correctly if the rider's weight does not complement that change, we should already be halfway there – at least in our understanding.

The higher airs

There is a very fine line between the preparation of the horse for passage and piaffe. Basically, we should not force either of these exercises but allow them to develop. This simply will not happen until the horse is sufficiently schooled and gymnastic enough to work in full collection. This has nothing to do with being drawn in by the bit; instead, the horse should be light in hand and energetic behind.

All the work achieved to date should have helped bring the horse to this position. It may, indeed should, have taken several years of patient, painstaking work. As a result, our horse will have developed noticable topline muscle, his abdominals will be toned, he will be laterally and longitudinally supple from nose to tail, and flexible through every joint. His hindlegs should be stepping well underneath him and he should be happy in a collected outline in walk, trot and canter. Once he has reached this state, he may be ready to move on to the higher airs, although it must be recognised that not all horses will ever realise their full potential – often because of mistakes made in the past or conformational setbacks.

Some horses find passage easier than piaffe, others the opposite. Whichever way it happens – more forward or upward bound and always a combination of both – it's a question of developing what's on offer. The horse himself will show us where and how his collection peaks, so whether it is on the spot, as in piaffe, or forward and up into passage, the exercises are a mere expression of the strength and confidence within.

In simple terms...

Passage is no more than a very candenced, very elevated trot. In passage, the diagonal gait is as much 'up' as forward and the horse appears suspended in his movement – the propulsion coming from the deeper engagement of the hindlimb joints.

Piaffe is even more collected and takes place on the spot. Most horses are capable of making passage and piaffe if they are 'hyped up' – say, horses at the start of a race. But to achieve this movement on demand requires a state of muscular strength and flexibility in the horse's back and hindquarters, which can only result from years of athletic development.

Although the subject is complex, riders who

have schooled their horses to a level where collection (without resistance) has become a way of life, may be ready to try for one or two steps at a time, then build up slowly.

Riding the movements

When it comes to riding passage and piaffe, we have to make ourselves as firm but as light as possible, which sounds like a contradiction in terms. Earlier in this book, we talked about sitting proud, puffing ourselves up, expanding the ribcage and making ourselves full of air, which in effect relieves the horse's back of stifling pressure. The truth is, whilst the balance of our bodies must be very stable, the horse will need as much freedom in his back as possible if he is to round his spine to the degree required for these very engaged exercises. Pushing down with the seat is therefore counterproductive. It's very much a question of sitting deeply, but

Towards piaffe. When the horse is able to halt and rein-back on soft reins, he will be more receptive to the seat and leg aids for piaffe and passage.

In halt, our legs move just behind the girth to close gently against the horse.

In rein-back we ask with the leg fractionally further back to activate each step. Here, Espada is in a nice frame, but his legs need to bend a little more to lower the haunches before we ask for piaffe.

This rein-back shows better flexion through the joints, although he is a little behind the bit for perfection.

Now the seat and leg must aid the diagonals to step on the spot without moving backward. Here, thinking 'forward', the outside hind is beginning to lift and flex nicely.

Here, the piaffe is established on the new diagonal pair, with both the outside fore and inside hind flexing and lifting. The moment the horse responds, ease the rein in reward.

For greater collection

(towards passage and piaffe)

To set the horse up for either movement, it is often helpful to ride a couple of steps of rein-back first, just to 'sit' the horse a little more on the hocks. The most important thing is that the horse is full of energy, but remains softly on the bit, with the poll forming roughly the highest point of the neck.

As we think forward again, whether in collected walk for piaffe or collected trot for passage, the feelings are similar. We should:

● ask and give a little more through the fingers, whilst still checking the pace through the elbows, shoulders and waist;

● keep both legs in the rein-back position, but release the pressure away from the horse's side by stretching down deeply with the heel (in the direction of the horse's hind heels);

● as the horse moves forward, apply feather-light taps behind the girth in the diagonal rhythm of the gait to 'stir up' impulsion;

● as you feel the power welling up under the saddle, feel that your seat and tummy only allow a certain amount 'through';

● now think of drawing more energy up with you by raising your diaphragm (remember, there must always be an outlet...) so the horse moves into your space.

In passage, we raise the diaphragm, lighten the seat, activate with the legs just behind the girth, and think forward and up!

102

supporting upwardly and proudly, so that we make room to take the horse up with us.

The aids for passage are therefore less about doing and more about allowing. Passage will often grow naturally out of the collected trot as the horse responds to nuances of rider position. The main change will be that once the horse is moving forward with controlled impulsion in collection, we simply lighten the weight of the back of the saddle by advancing the waist, stretching tall and gently moving the legs further back. This action should come from the rider's hips rather than from the knee down, to enable the whole leg to move back as though reaching down to 'gather' the horse's hind feet.

Although you may bring your shoulders slightly forward of the vertical, be careful not to collapse in front – it's the tone of the rider's abdominal muscles which retains the balance and provides the horse with the upward support required. Basically, the rider's bodyweight should now be placed closer to the pommel, which will help free the horse's rounding back.

In applying these aids, try to imagine what the horse is feeling. Bringing the legs back not only transfers weight to the haunches, it brings a gentle weight aid to bear through the front of the seat. This has the effect of dampening forward progression. Therefore, by narrowing the gap through which the horse should flow, this gently applied seat aid will help to re-channel much of the energy upwards.

The most important thing in developing these movements is not to use force. It is the horse that gives the power to us, not the other way round. We may shake the contents of the bottle, but the bubbles and fizz come from within, and then it's up to us how much we ease the cork!

Always reward

Once we allow the leg to drop forward again to its normal position of toe aligned with the girth (see Chapter Two) and relax the tummy muscles, we naturally release the horse out of this very collected posture. Don't forget either that in the beginning, every step of passage or piaffe should be rewarded by relaxing all pressure and giving with the hand. Stroking and words of praise work wonders. Then the horse will want to do it again, and we can put more steps together.

What can go wrong?

● **The horse shoots backwards.** After the rein-back, the horse must always go forward; he can only do this if we release! Remember, passage and piaffe are both forward movements, so our aids must make this clear. Soften your tummy muscles or ease the shoulders back if in difficulty.

● **The horse shuffles about and the quarters swing out.** An uneven seat or too much leg aid (sideways pressure) will unbalance the horse. Your legs move back to transfer weight to the haunches, not to push him about.

● **The horse tries to dive forward.** You have forgotten to contain some of the energy with your upper body, particularly through the abdominals and shoulders. Stretch down more through the front of the thigh, and up more through the front of your waist.

● **You can feel something happening behind, but the front feet are planted.** Your horse is probably leaning on you. Give and take with both hands so he can't lean; then touch him lightly with the dressage stick behind the leg to keep the hindlegs under; this should lighten the forehand.

● **Your horse seems to be trying, but feels very flat.** Sit up more, feel your ankle joints soften whilst your hip joints and thighs open around the horse (knees and toes still pointing forwards) and think open seat, open shoulders, open mind!

Before you try...

... consider the following points:

● Does my horse work through from behind and offer impulsion when requested?

● Does my horse accept my hand and remain 'on the bit' with an arched neck, without leaning?

● Does my horse feel 'up' and rounded through the back, and is the poll the highest point of his body?

● Do I know how to 'lighten' my seat and take pressure off the back of the saddle?

● Am I able to halt or rein-back from the seat and leg with a mere feel on the rein?

● Does my horse balance himself and come 'more together' when I sit proudly?

● Is there more elevation nowadays in his natural gaits?

● Can I achieve collection on light reins?

If you can honestly answer yes to all these questions, then you are probably ready to introduce your horse to piaffe and passage. If not, your horse is clearly not yet in self-carriage and it would be a mistake to attempt this too early, since you may end up hollowing him, which is a common fault.

Another good sign of strength and balance is when you can work the horse deep, whilst his back and wither remains 'up' and supported so that he can take the contact forward and downward, without leaning on your hand.

The secret of success

One of the great secrets to achieve a successful passage is to understand that the taller you sit, the more your centre of gravity comes up. Once the horse feels this he will – if he has been schooled to follow his rider – want to move into the same orbit. In simple terms, this means he will attempt to merge himself with you by raising the entire forehand upward as the hindlegs move deeper underneath and lift the whole. Invisible riding is all about these subtle changes of posture. How the horse feels our weight will change with every tiny movement we make.

I hope this book has made things a little clearer for you and you can now recognise that there is nothing artificial about the methods described in these pages. Every conventional aid involves changes of weight and pressure, but too often this is not understood, which is why things can go so badly wrong. The weight aids are the most natural in the world, and constitute the horseman's greatest tools.

As with all tools, however, they need to be handled with care; if we don't respect them, they can work against us. Generally, though, our horse will tell us when we get it right. If we take the trouble, he may even thank us by showing us marvellous things.

It takes very good balance and strength in the horse's back and quarters to hold a collected frame on the circle for several strides on a light rein. Once you can achieve this, however, your horse should be ready to attempt the higher airs.

Piaffe – ridden outdoors adds lightness and zest to this very natural movement.

Passage – spontaneously offered outside is an expression of contained energy, strength behind, and joy.

Chapter Eleven

Outside the manège

Most riders will admit that dressage should form part of the training of the horse for any competitive discipline. Wherever precision, economy and time comes into the equation, most agree it could be irresponsible to avoid schooling prior to setting forth to an event, show jumping class or hunter trials. But what about other disciplines? Surely these can exist quite happily without having to know all these rather intricate details about downward pressure and centering oneself, etc?

Lasting success?

The elegant pastime of top class showing has existed for decades and managed very well long before dressage became so popular! But dressage does come into it, even if under a different name. People produce good, often brilliant, horses for a number of disciplines without ever having a dressage lesson in their lives, and certainly never having read about the methods described in this book. However, you can be fairly sure that the most successful have been using the same principles naturally, and probably quite unconsciously, for many years. As already stated, there have always existed highly talented natural horsemen and women throughout the world. But that doesn't mean the rest of us do not need help.

Let me reiterate that the methodology of invisible riding, tuning into Nature's laws and learning how to use our own bodyweight to bring about a response in the horse, should appear supremely natural and effortless – by the very fact that it is inbuilt! In the same way that the toddler learns to walk, run, jump, skip, hop and do the things that children do, we should eventually become as natural in the saddle as we are on the ground.

Once you've been shown the way and a

knowledge of the theory can be added to the practice, the success rate can be multiplied many times over. Ultimately, the idea is that the more you do, the more it will all become second nature to you and the horse.

How horses like to ridden

Riding naturally is exactly what we are talking about here - invisible aiding! This means:
- invisible changes of weight and pressure on the horse's back;
- invisible invitations at the horse's side;
- invisible nudges against the horse's side;
- invisible gives and takes on the rein;
- invisible lightening or deepening of the seat;

....and so on, ad infinitum. And once we take all that on board and understand that this is the way horses like to be ridden, the improvement will be marked.

So is this book only for dressage riders? On the contrary, it's for all riders. The horse is still a horse and a rider is still a rider, so it doesn't matter what kind of riding you wish to do. Whether you're competitive or non-competitive, whether you hack, hunt, event, or play polo, we are all bound by the same laws of nature and by the same physical and mental constraints. But what we need to know is how to work with and around these. The natural aids I have described in this book work for every rider – whatever shape or size – and every horse – whatever breed or type. They also work in every situation

The horse who is constantly praised and taught through positive reinforcement will give his all (and more) in everything he does.

– in or outside the arena, in the countryside or walking along the road, and so on.

Safety

These riding techniques should produce a safer rider and a safer horse. Why? Because the seat is more balanced and the methods themselves complement the way in which the horse moves, so there should be no stress or upset. Your horse should begin to feel much happier within himself once you have learned the techniques of invisible riding. He will begin to feel more at one with you, and once he can relate to you in a way which is natural to you both, he will want to please you. Where a command becomes a request, becomes a whisper, becomes a thought... all this makes for a much more balanced, controlled way of riding – and all achieved through co-operation and partnership rather than force and restraint.

Let us now look at some scenarios, and refer back to the various chapters which will most help in these various scenarios.

Hacking out

For me personally I can think of nothing more pleasant than hacking a horse which is light on my hand, forward going and happy in whichever gait I ask him to go. If he is responsive to my weight aids I will feel even better, knowing that if I encounter any sort of problem I can turn away easily, move back if required, or ride boldly past.

At the other end of the scale, I can think of nothing less pleasant than hacking out on a horse which jogs when I want to walk, and either pulls or disdains to go forward when I want to trot and canter. The horse that is heavy on the hand will be harder to manoeuvre; it can become a battle of wills to change direction and do something simple like closing a gate. Since the whole idea of riding should be that the horse carries you, it can be extremely tiring on the rider's back and shoulders if the horse leans on the rein. It can also be dangerous if you are unable to stop easily and in balance at a moment's notice.

Horse on the forehand

How can this be changed? The leaning horse should soon learn to carry himself if you give him some basic schooling work on circles and turns, and gradually introduce a little leg yield or shoulder-in for a few strides. If not for dressage, these need not be text-book perfect, but the very act of bending from nose to tail and being asked to step laterally will teach him to transfer more weight to the hocks (and less on your hand), and quarter-pirouettes are invaluable for this work, too. It will also teach you control of the quarters, which is vital when riding in company or with other road users.

You certainly don't need a manège to teach any of these things; the lateral work can be taught on a path or track and the bending work in any open space. Work in walk on a hard surface will do no harm at all and the seeds of lightening the forehand will be sown. More important is always to be able to straighten up and go forward again, and there is no reason at all why you should not do all this out hacking. Indeed, simple exercises like these can work wonders, especially when you make the straightening up part seem like a reward for the more demanding bend and yield work.

Idle horse

On a lazy horse, the rider must take time to sensitise him to the on-off or press-and-release aspect of the leg aids. This will sharpen his senses which have been dulled from too much squeeze, squeeze, squeeze, or even thud, thud, thud in the past (see Chapter One).

Long distance riding

Most of the points covered in the preceding three paragraphs will equally apply here. The posture of the rider, with the bodyweight carried in balance aided by supple joints, can make an enormous difference to the long-distance horse. No matter how fit the horse, a sloppy or heavy seat will impact more and this will gradually debilitate him the further the distance travelled. Learning to balance in the stirrups, easing the weight through the joints, and employing the various methods described in this book will all combine to spare the horse's back. In this way, he has a much better chance of using the full range of his capabilities, economise on effort and arrive at his destination less tired and in better shape than his badly ridden counterpart.

Downhill shouldn't mean on the forehand! How much safer we will be on a straight, supple and balanced mount.

Although in this form of riding we do not want to collect the horse, we do want him to use his hindlegs to full advantage. Pushing from behind leads to freedom of the shoulder, which allows longer, more sweeping strides in front; this can only be developed once the horse has learned to bring his hocks more underneath him. For this reason, taking time to teach him how to do so will reap huge benefits all round.

Cross country

Even at intermediate event level, it's not unusual to see riders struggling to keep their horses in check before a jump, or to make a swift change of direction. Of course, there will always be explosive horses and I am not suggesting that there are any easy answers for a very hot, excitable type. Nevertheless, some riders use their seats in such a way that they tend to exacerbate the problem rather than relieve it. In Chapter Three I described the technique of 'letting the weight down' which involves making yourself very centred and gently blocking the horse through the strongest part of his body, rather than over the more sensitive areas of his back. We discussed this in relation to the downward transitions and at a higher level in the piaffe and passage work in Chapter Nine.

Choosing how much energy to allow 'through' before a tricky combination of jumps, or even to effect a better turn into a jump, can make all the difference when riding cross country. Using our bodyweight effectively gives us a wonderful gearbox where we may steady or slow whilst raising the 'revs' at the same time. Free-wheeling round a course of jumps is not the answer, we want the energy, but we also need to know how to harness it.

Learning, therefore, how to 'contain' your horse in the same way as we did in collection, by checking through the abdominals and taking the weight down into the thighs, knees and stirrups (kept well underneath you), will keep the horse in a much better balance – even when cantering on or in full gallop.

Unfortunately, too many riders give the horse conflicting aids by pulling back and then leaning back at the same time. Consider this downward spiral of events:

● **leaning back generally pushes the horse more forward;**
● **the seatbones dig into the loins and create hollowing;**
● **the horse's head comes up as he tries to move away from the discomfort;**
● **the rider's hands come up as they try to check;**
● **high hands destroy upper body balance and the feet shoot forward;**
● **the rider is now totally out of balance;**
● **any sense of centering or 'grounding' through gravity is lost;**
● **the horse is stronger than his rider and the whole thing escalates into a tug-of-war.**

Yes one can – in some cases – stop a horse through the mouth, but it is a very ill-advised thing to do since it will make the horse harder and harder through the bars of the mouth each time it happens. Gadgets or stronger bits only have a very temporary effect, and it would be so much better for everyone if the problem could be cured at source.

A bubbly, excited horse like Elaine's stallion, feeling that spring has come, responds immediately to the dampening down position of her legs and seat, as learned in Chapter Three.

Too hot to handle

Whenever I find myself on a very flighty, hot-blooded or sensitive horse, I try to stay clear of doing anything which might aggravate his back. Instead, I generally lighten my seat by taking a more forward position with hollowed loins and firm tummy, and then transfer all the weight down through my thighs, knees and inner calves.

Bridging the reins is very helpful as, instead of pulling against the horse's mouth, I simply apply downward pressure on the 'bridge' itself. This steadies the forehand and complements

Bridging the reins, as here, can be helpful when riding a hot horse, as the action is not directly on the horse's mouth.

the checking effect of more downward pressure into the stirrups. Since all this affects the horse over his centre of gravity he soon learns it's a waste of energy to pull against himself. Once he gives up trying to take off, one can then start to sit a little more into him, and after a while, just the bracing of the tummy and loin muscles and the weighting of the stirrups alone may be enough to persuade him.

Another method to reduce pulling, is to give with one rein or the other as appropriate (but never with both unless you're very confident). Beware also of 'to-ing and fro-ing' with the contact. Take up the contact with both hands in the normal way and then, whilst one rein retains its normal feel, try giving softly forward with the other. Once the horse discovers there is less support in front, he will feel the need to support himself elsewhere – from behind.

Out in open country there should be nothing to stop you riding a curve whichever way you are going. If caught out in the middle of a field, for example, with a very strong horse, take time to ride around the area, rather than aiming straight across. Horses are like arrows, the straighter the aim, the swifter they become. Don't give the horse the chance to flatten out and savour his own strength. Keep him soft and manoeuvrable by bending him gently on a big curve, feel that he is always slightly around one leg or the other (remember our 'grounding' pillar) and retain him there by letting your weight drop down. Doing this a few times on both reins out on exercise can work wonders. Again, only release your horse out of the bend to ride forward when he has stopped pulling.

Showjumping
There is no doubt that a light, nimble, flexible horse will win hands down in any form of precision jumping competition – provided his jump is as good as the rest of him! Taking trouble to school your horse prior to jumping will give you that edge, particularly regarding quick turns, and getting round the course without time faults.

You need not do anything too fancy to improve performance. Circles and turns will be of particular benefit and always, when wanting quick reactions, use the outside leg to turn your horse into a jump as explained in Chapter Five. Not only does this have the benefit of turning him more from behind, but the outside leg can guard him from running out and missing a jump

altogether!

Ride as much as possible in the stirrups. If approaching a jump, feel how you can straighten up much more quickly, not with the rein but with your weight. If you feel you are not coming in quite centrally and the horse is bearing too much right, don't interfere with the front end or you risk a run out. Instead, act on the centre of your horse, transfer more pressure into your left stirrup and he will be straight again. It's just a question of balancing those scales we read about in Chapter Five.

Western riding
Western riding is the one discipline where the use of the indirect rein and weight aids are generally talked about ad infinitum. A good Western seat is not unlike the classical seat of the Spanish Riding School, and is very centred. A bad Western seat is as bad as a bad hunting seat, where the rider leans against the cantle, stirrups thrust forward and the horse has to carry too much pressure on the weakest part of his back.

The idea of the long stirrup in Western riding was based originally on the riding of the Mexicans, whose methods had been handed down from the time of the Spanish conquistadors. The idea was to ride crotch deep in the saddle for security and to give weight aids over the horse's strongest point!

In Western riding, the weight aids will be so much more effective when the rider sits tall, upright and balanced. If the long stirrup makes this difficult, it may be necessary to shorten it to that point where the rider can let the weight down without his or her balance slipping back. Lunge lessons on a blanket with no stirrups will be most helpful to confirm and centralise the seat.

There is no doubt that good Western riders can move their horses easily and seamlessly this way and that without any obvious movement. This all goes to show that invisible riding methods are very much alive in other areas.

Riding on or near busy roads
We all like to have a straight horse, but we must never confuse stiffness with straightness. Since the quarters are wider than the forehand, it is taking a risk not to have some knowledge of how to bend and how to move the whole horse into the side if a large vehicle comes towards

Without a degree of bend, it can be difficult to stay into the verge. Suppling your hacking horse is hugely worthwhile.

us. Anxious to get themselves out of trouble, some people actually put themselves more at risk by tugging on the wrong rein. On a stiff, unsettled or spooking horse, tugging to the left takes the forehand left, but generally swings the quarters right – out into the traffic, with possible disastrous consequences.

The same principle goes for the spooky horse who is always looking for flapping plastic or rubbish in the hedgerow. Never face him into these distractions – that's just asking for trouble! Instead, think of a little shoulder-in to get him past (see Chapter Seven). Always let him bend or face towards the centre of the road so he can concentrate on you rather than possible hidden dangers lurking at the side. In both these scenarios, it is absolutely vital that you remember the principle of one side of your body acting, whilst the other allows. Too many people tense up all round, use equal amounts of leg and rein to regain control and wonder why their horse stews and hots up under them. So think logically and act as herd leader. A quiet, sure attitude from you will lend confidence and calm your horse.

Pony Club, gymkhana games etc

By now the reader may have come to appreciate that invisible riding works for everyone. One of my most successful videos to date has been *Staying On*, which features children of different abilities riding their ponies. None of the ponies which participated in the film were dressage trained, but all had done basic Pony Club and riding school work.

In the video, each child's performance improved drastically once they were introduced to some of the techniques described in this book. Several children had problems with the canter, because they had failed to 'let go' and use the inside leg like a pillar. By showing them how to stabilise and deepen the inside leg, they could not only achieve the correct strike off, they could also keep the canter going for much longer and without more effort.

They also learned how their ponies could become more forward going simply by sitting tall and allowing the pony to round up underneath them. They learned to stop by sitting up but 'closing down'.

Some young pupils told me afterwards how

Safe on the roads

To 'tuck in', we must first achieve bend to the right. If we can do this, we can then control the quarters just as we learned to do in turn on the forehand, leg-yield and shoulder-in (right). The aids are clearly given in Chapter Seven.

It is working the horse from the inside-out that secures his position on the verge. To sum up therefore:

● feel gently or open the right rein to ask the horse to look more into the road – you should just see his right eye and the rim of his nostril a little more;

● stimulate bend with your inside (right) leg at the girth; keep the outside leg fairly passive;

● once your horse is bending to the right, apply more pressure at the girth with the right leg – think weight-against or leg yield to nudge him into the verge — whilst gently opening the left rein;

● you should now have control of the quarters.

● To secure the forehand, keep him looking right by squeezing the fingers; then gently close the right rein against the base of the neck (don't cross it!);

● to move in that extra inch, sit momentarily a little more on the outside seatbone or step more into the outside stirrup and open the outside left rein again;

● now hold him there by sitting quietly, central and proud, right leg like a pillar;

● talk to him in a calming voice and, when it is safe, move off the verge and ride forward again;

All this may sound complicated, but it only takes a second or two and should become second nature. We must have control of the whole horse, forehand and quarters, when riding on the road, but the secret is to bend him through the middle and maintain it.

An exaggerated use of inside leg to outside hand will be invaluable for riding a young or inexperienced horse along the road. Here, we see with Mary and Prazer how good schoolwork will improve safety when they venture out.

the technique of riding correctly in the stirrups had improved their gymkhana games – musical poles, bending races and zigzags – they simply dropped their weight fractionally to the required side and hey presto – the effect was instantaneous! One or two had started polo, and found the same principles worked there too.

Parents were pleased too, especially those who had become frustrated watching their children using too much hand and tugging on their ponies' mouths. One mother wrote to me to say she felt her daughter was ruining her pony's mouth, but now her riding was transformed as she thought about riding 'the other way round'.

In conclusion

To sum up therefore, invisible riding is for all riders in any and all circumstances. It simply comprises a language via which the horse can respond in the most immediate way possible. Once the horse feels us make this effort to work at his level, he will be much more willing to give us what we want. For the first time perhaps he will be able to act without compromising his own precious balance. At last, he too will feel safe. So think forward and up - and ride on!

Confidence has to be a two-way partnership.

Chapter Twelve

Questions and answers

Q My four-year-old has only recently been backed. He is an Arab and very sensitive with a high head carriage. I'm afraid riding with weight aids might be too much for him.

A First, let me explain – we're not talking about creating more weight or pressure on the horse's back, we're simply learning how to manage it. Riders who never consider how and where they balance can really add to the burden. We all weigh something and can't get away from that fact, but I'm teaching you how to make small adjustments in everything you do, which will make life easier – not more difficult – for your horse.

Arabs are lovely, intelligent, sensitive horses and respond to this way of training extremely well; the more subtle you are, the better. As for any young horse, since they have never had the chance to be confused or desensitised by forceful riding methods, the weight aids will work for them in a much more immediate way. After all, we are simply working here with the horse's natural impulses; not introducing commands that will need to be learned and re-learned, long before he can understand.

The wonderful thing about this way of riding, is the fact it will heighten your own awareness, make you much more sensitive to your horse's needs, and make the correct response much

Arabs, Thoroughbreds and many Irish horses, like Milo here, will hollow away from too much seat in the early days.

By adopting a light seat for all forward work, and gradually introducing bend and stretch exercises as the horse becomes more confident, acceptance of the aids will develop in a harmonious, unstressed way.

more accessible. The beauty of it all is that you can then set the horse up in such a way that he thinks it was his idea in the first place!

With the newly backed horse, my only caveat about the weight aids will concern those of the seat, since these should not be applied until the horse is stronger under saddle. Of course, every horse is different, but Arabs and Thoroughbreds usually have very sensitive backs so, from the beginning, adopt a light forward seat, balancing in your stirrups as much as possible. You can still practise your 'opening up' to go forward, and 'closing down' for downward transitions through your abdominals in this position.

Do plenty of outdoor riding if you can, and try not to interfere too much with the mouth at this stage. Don't worry unduly if the head comes up and your horse pokes his nose at first. Just establish a light, elastic contact and, as he learns to use his hind end more and strengthens through the back, things will get better.

When schooling, go for big circles with lots of straight work in between, remembering that no horse can be really straight until he is equally supple on both reins. To help with this, teach him to move gently away as well as more around your leg. That is the first big step towards bringing him towards accepting the bit. Do not ask for circles in trot until he understands what you want in walk. Never spend too much time in one gait. Young horses need plenty of breaks and a lot of stretch work if they are going to build muscle in the correct places. Once he starts to pile on that dorsal muscle, any hollowing or head problems should gradually diminish.

Q **Why does riding more in the stirrups help the horse? Surely our weight will stay the same whether we're sitting or rising?**

A This is a common misunderstanding. It has become the fashion to sit into the young horse far too early. Also, people often spend too long in sitting trot without giving the horse a break; dressage tests do not give us much option after a certain level. Even an advanced horse needs space and we should aim to free the back by riding rising trot in between the more collected or extended work where sitting deeper can stimulate forward progression once the back can take it.

The truth is, we need to get off the horse's

With or without stirrups, the horse can cope with our weight so much better when we sit up and simply allow our legs to fall away from us. We can then replace the stirrups, which will help us adjust and free the horse's back from unwanted pressure, as and when appropriate.

back as much as we sit into it if he is to build good topline. Muscles, like joints, get tired, and too much sitting into the horse cramps the blood flow, which deprives the muscles of sugar and basically reduces their ability to grow! When we use the stirrups, the horse will obviously still feel our weight, but it is transferred to – and carried by – the very strongest part of his back, over that part where the stirrups are slung. This minimises the pressure over the spine and relieves the weaker areas.

In the light, or forward seat used for jumping, we balance more on the inner thighs. This again spares the back and spreads the weight of the rider more over the horse's sides. All this will encourage him to engage more behind since he no longer feels a heavy pressure behind and under the seat of the saddle.

Although the amplification of the gaits in a well-schooled horse can be helped by temporarily sitting more into him and 'driving' him forward from behind by bringing the shoulders back, the effect is shortlived once the back muscles get tired. There are other ways of increasing the length of stride and I would suggest we use both to get the best out of our horses. Rising to the trot with a feeling of leading from the sternum is very effective. By raising our centre of gravity in this way, the horse responds by lightening his forehand and raising his own centre of gravity. This allows greater scope for the hindlegs.

Try never to collapse your abdominals when you rise to the trot, think of a good forward jumping seat, then reduce the angle and feel you are nicely balanced over your stirrups, preserving the angles of the leg so the ball of the foot, as well as the knees, act as a spring. Provided you keep your back slightly braced, never rounded, riding more in the stirrups can do wonders for all the gaits.

Q **If invisible riding is so good, is there any need for sticks and spurs?**

A Certainly the techniques described in this book should make you much more self-reliant as a rider. Hopefully, it will remove the need to use any running reins or gadgets for outline, since all the emphasis is about riding the horse from back to front, rather than the other way round. However, the conventional aids of dressage stick and spur may continue to be useful, depending very much on the nature of the horse. As a matter of principle I always carry a

Espada is the only horse in my stable whom I generally ride with spurs. Here, my right leg momentarily applies the spur to ask for greater crossing behind in half-pass left.

stick, but since this is very much used to help the horse and never as a chastisement, I see it merely as an extension of the natural aids.

The stick is particularly helpful to indicate to the hind end to tuck itself more under in, say, the collected gaits, or to encourage the horse to move over more swiftly with one hindleg or the other in the lateral movements. Although it does induce impulsion, I try rarely to use it to ask the horse to move more quickly since for me, going forward has much more to do with allowing than 'making'. A well-trained horse should hopefully want to move!

However, there will always be exceptions and this is where the use of the spur as a subtle adjunct to the leg aids is useful. Spurs should never be applied (as is too often seen) in every stride. The idea is to give a very quick, light aid with the spur to introduce an element of surprise. Used in this way to create an extra and immediate request for impulsion or reach of the hindlegs is acceptable. Used all the time in conjunction with the legs is counterproductive. The horse will become as inured and dead to the spur as he is to the leg, and what then? Moderation is the name of the game when it comes to any aid, especially the artificial ones. Of all the horses in my stable, only one horse is ridden with spurs and during a half-hour schooling session, I probably would only apply them about about two dozen times and then literally, just an 'ask', never a dig or a scrape. No one should wear spurs until they have complete control of their legs and know the difference in feel between an impulsion aid and a closing down aid. Otherwise, we will do far more harm than good.

I have always envied those riders whose legs can encircle the horse's barrel (above) without appearing to float in mid air as mine seem to! (below)

Q **I've always envied people with long legs for riding. I'm of the short square build, and my legs only come halfway down the horse's sides. What hope is there of invisible riding for me?**

A Every hope, especially once you've developed a good seat. Having taught many people built as you are, I've never encountered a problem – often the opposite – since shorter people seem more in touch with their own centre of gravity. This has made it much easier for my schoolmasters to understand them, provided their balance is correct.

The point is, whatever our shape or size, we are all influenced by the same natural laws and

provided we learn to marry our centre of gravity with that of the horse, everything else will fall into place. Generally I have found 'square' riders sit more quietly, too. This gives the horse a chance to balance under them since there is less temptation to collapse the waist (a favourite with willowy people), rock with the shoulders or flay about with long, uncontrollable legs. That is why for the higher airs, slim people need to 'puff' themselves up more to give the horse a feeling of core stability. I'll never forget meeting that riding legend Nuno Oliveira for the first time. I'd often seen him ride, and had thought him to be a big man with a massive torso. Imagine my surprise when this surprisingly slight figure came towards me on his own two feet and shook my hand.

As regards leg position, it may appear easier to aid on the girth for the long legged person, but the aid itself is about stimulating nerve endings relating to the intercostal nerve. Since there are just as many of these, possibly more, higher up on the girth, it shouldn't matter too much the exact position - as long as the leg does not stray back. Obviously, a longer stirrup leather will help the rider to support at the forehand whether short or long in the leg, and if the rider is not sitting on the three point seat, it will be very difficult to allow the weight of the leg to 'drop' down – which is important.

Finally, don't envy people with my length of leg. On a lazy horse, I find it very difficult to give meaningful aids for impulsion, and spurs are basically useless since only by cocking the leg up at an extreme angle backwards can they come into contact with the horse's skin!

Q You say the weight aids should be subtle. My 16.3hh Warmblood gelding is very stiff to the right – and I have even tried standing in the right stirrup on circles and he still refuses to bend into my leg!

A I'm not surprised – drastic shifts of weight would make any horse nervous to attempt anything! In each and every exercise, we must try to feel what the horse feels from us in order to understand why they can or cannot do something. In your case, standing into the inside right stirrup is bound to make your inside leg so hard and stiff that he will feel blocked by it. It may also cause your right seatbone to push against him, rather than opening downwards around him. On a right circle, it's always a

A little sideways pressure from the inside seatbone, knee and thigh will often improve bend, whilst the lower leg asks in a more subtle way – allowing as well as asking.

balancing act between inviting the horse to move a little more inward and around your leg and keeping him 'out' to the circle. So too much one way or the other will be counterproductive.

When I want more bend, I almost have the feeling of moulding plasticine with my leg. Whilst there is fractionally more pressure in my inside stirrup and inside seatbone, I make tiny nudgey feels with my inside leg against the girth. The idea is to soften and to bend the middle of the horse away from me – which will bring the extremities a little more inward and around my leg. This is a very different feeling from the horse falling in through the inside shoulder or falling in through the inside hindleg. It simply means that on a circle, the hindlegs can follow in the tracks of the forelegs without deviation. In other words, the horse moulds itself into the shape of the circle.

Often, when teaching, I see riders try very hard with the inside lower leg to bend the horse and retain the circumference of the circle but, despite sitting very evenly, the horse drifts more and more inward.

"Am I collapsing to the inside?" they ask in despair. *"I don't feel I am, but I can't stop him spiralling inward. What am I doing wrong?"* The answer when we look becomes obvious. The basic seat may be correct but the horse is 'escaping' to the inside because he has found a gap lower down. Remember we talked about the horse always finding the way out, or the weakest part of our body? This works for us when we deliberately make room, but can work against us when we don't mean it.

In the case of the rider I've just described, I see that an over-industrious inside lower leg has allowed the inside knee and thigh to gape open. To keep the horse bending but staying 'out' to the circle, they will need instead to keep the inside hip forward, and to close the thigh and knee against the saddle. Indeed, a well-schooled horse can be kept 'out' to the circle (whatever the size, 20, 15 or 10 metres or even less) with a gentle pressure from the thigh alone.

Remember, this must never involve gripping; it's the weight of the rider's leg that keeps the horse out, or brings him in. What most riders need is more muscle tone through the thighs in order to be more efficient with the lower leg aids. We should be able to lift the lower leg away from the knee to apply an aid without losing the stability of the thigh. As I wrote in *The Classical Seat* – think of the upper leg as part of the seat and once we do this our leg aids can become much more effective and quiet.

It's important always to remember too the position of the hips must be correct (inside hip slightly in advance of the outside hip on a turn or circle), since they give support and flexibility to the leg below.

Remember – horses will always pick up on our weaknesses which creates problems in them. By increasing your own muscle tone (with exercises off the ground when not riding) on your weaker side as well as your stronger, you will greatly help your horse to develop his muscle tone more evenly. It will be well worth it.

Sylvia explains the use of the whole leg and why the knee and thigh should softly envelop the horse.

Q I have a 15-year-old, rather stodgy 14.3hh cob mare. She has gone on her forehand all of her life and I feel it is rather late to teach her new tricks. Would you agree?

A The answer has to be no – since it should never be too late to improve any human or equine posture, unless there are biomechanical reasons for leaving well alone. Provided she is not arthritic or sore through the back, I see no reason why you should not help your mare find a better balance. Although this will take time and patience, since she has been used to going in a certain way for so long, I believe it would be much better and nicer for her in the end.

Fifteen is not so old, and one of the great

Here is a photograph of my Lusitano mare, Andorinha, taken at roughly the same age as your horse. She too likes to go on her forehand and, having been a brood mare, was only broken at eight years old. Teaching her new tricks has, however, been a life saver; she is still fit and active at 24, despite various setbacks. My vet says that learning collected work saved her forelimbs which had threatened to give up!.

advantages of working the horse from behind is it can make them feel young again. Not only does it spare the forelimbs, it allows the back to work properly through greater engagement behind, and should lead to a much longer working life. We need only consider the horses of the Spanish Riding School, some still featuring in performances well into their late twenties, to see that this is true.

Of course, you will need to take things step-by-step. However, we have to do this anyway with young horses so it is not so very different. Where you will benefit is already having the horse's confidence and, hopefully, a good relationship. The first step towards bringing the horse off the forehand is, as always, introducing bend. Do this through the usual circle and turn work and build up gradually as explained in the preceding chapters. Spiralling down from a big circle to a smaller one is a very good way of teaching the older horse to transfer more weight behind. As each inside hindleg will want to step more under the horse's frame for balance, a gradual lightening of the shoulders will emerge. In fact, in some cases, an older horse can find this really liberating and thrilling and get a new lease of life.

When I teach people with older horses, I generally ride the horses first in order to advise on their stiffnesses and difficulties. Often, I am amazed how much the horse is prepared to offer, although they have never been asked for these things before. Work with your horse therefore, treat her like a youngster initially, and then see how much she's prepared to offer you. You may be pleasantly surprised!

Q **I can't see that adjusting the balance will make so much difference as you say. Surely if the horse is carrying 150lbs, he's still carrying 150lbs?**

A I've already explained that *where* the horse carries our weight can make all the difference to him. As for *how*, we need only to turn back to Chapter Two to see that a slumped person feels much heavier than a person who sits up and takes responsibility for their own weight.

I've never done much ballroom dancing but I'm told on good authority that some of the largest, heaviest male dancers are the lightest on their feet. This is because they have learned to deal with and manage those extra pounds in good balance. They are so light that they can twirl their female partners almost round their little finger. That's rather like a good centred rider, working a horse on the lightest of reins.

Looking at it from another angle, when I ran a large dressage academy with my late husband, we used to have a middle-aged gentleman who came for riding lessons. He tried terribly hard, but despite his best efforts seemed to leave all our horses exhausted at the end of their lesson. One horse became almost lame when he rode it and we kept putting him on bigger and stronger horses until finally we found one who could just about sustain him without creeping back to the stable looking virtually arthritic.

We could never quite understand why he should bring about this effect. Admittedly, he was stiff but being only about an inch taller than me and fairly trim in shape, it was all quite a mystery. In the end we put it down to really heavy bones. At that time our weight limit at the stables was 168lbs so we imagined he must be on the verge of this and, coupled with his stiffness, just too much for most of our horses.

Long after our big stable closed down, he applied to me for lessons again. By this time I only owned two (not so young) schoolmasters and had a strict weight limit of 147lbs. I felt confident of putting him off when I told him this. He was jubilant, *"….but that's exactly what I weigh!"* he said, *"when may I come?"*

I was completely taken aback. I could only assume that, despite his actual bodyweight, he sat so heavily and in such a constricting way that he made the horse feel it was being bowed down by a huge, unpleasant burden. Fortunately, circumstances changed and he never came, but it was a great lesson to me in how some people make light work of their bodyweight and others can be so destructive. I guess that is why I have written this book. I now see that the balancing of our bodies is absolutely fundamental to the horse's wellbeing, ability and happiness.

But perhaps it is not so surprising and revelationary as some would assume. After all, if we ourselves are out of balance on the ground, what hope would there be for us to perform the most simple athletic task? When in doubt, always put yourself in the position of the horse and you will be surprised and heartened how much you both improve.

Good luck!

Riding with invisible aids makes for a much happier, more attentive horse. The feeling of joy is equally shared.

Author's acknowledgments

Many thanks to all those students who were kind enough to act and appear as guinea pigs in the putting together of this book. Namely Suzanne Bratton, Lizzie Fielden, Elaine Herbert, Mary O'Kane, Ruth Berril and my daughter Allegra - now a fully fledged university student. Also to Arlene Crawford for turning out our beloved horses to her usual high standard, and to Melanie Wilkes, Annie Wright and my husband Richard, for general support and backup.

If it were not for Kate Austin and Alison Bridge as well as you, the readers of **HORSE&RIDER**, this book would never have been written. I owe all the D J Murphy team a huge debt for their belief and enthusiasm, and particularly to my editor, Janet Rising, for her tireless hard work, good humour and meticulous eye for detail.

About the author

Sylvia Loch enjoyed a conventional British equestrian background before going to work in Portugal where she lived for 10 years, captivated by the horses and the opportunity to study High School. In 1979, Lord and Lady Loch returned to England to open the Lusitano Stud and Equitation Centre – the first academy of its kind in the UK. Not long after Lord Loch's death, Sylvia began to write for *Horse & Rider* magazine. Her popular *Classical Seat* series culminated in a book of the same name. First published in 1988, this is still an international bestseller. *Invisible Riding* is her latest title, and is based on her more recent *Horse and Rider* magazine series, *Weight Aids Demystified*, and *Virtual Riding*.

Now remarried to Richard Hawkins, Sylvia rides, teaches and trains at her Scottish Borders yard, attracting students from all over the world, eager to learn on her Lusitano schoolmasters. Her other books, *The Royal Horse of Europe, Dressage – the Art of Equitation, The Classical Rider* and *Dressage in Lightness*, have brought international renown. Founder of the Lusitano Breed Society of Great Britain and of the Classical Riding Club, Sylvia's website at www.classical-dressage.net is available to all interested in the classical principles of riding, and she has now made a series of best-selling videos based on her writing.